A
CARROT
A DAY

A CARROT A DAY

A daily dose of RECOGNITION
for your employees

ADRIAN GOSTICK
AND CHESTER ELTON

with
Greg Boswell
and
Scott Christopher

GIBBS
P
SMITH

Gibbs Smith, Publisher
Salt Lake City

This book is dedicated to the memory of Obert Clark Tanner, a man who dedicated his life to the study of appreciation. Obert never let a day pass without valuing those around him. You could say he was the first practitioner of the Carrot a Day philosophy.

19 18 17 16 15   24 23 22 21 20

Text © 2004 O. C. Tanner Company

Published by
Gibbs Smith, Publisher
P.O. Box 667
Layton, Utah 84041

Orders: 1.800.748.5439
www.gibbs-smith.com

Designed by Gotham Design
Printed and bound in Korea

Library of Congress Cataloging-in-Publication Data
Gostick, Adrian Robert.

A carrot a day : a daily dose of recognition for your employees / by Adrian Gostick and Chester Elton ; with Greg Boswell and Scott Christopher—1st ed.
p. cm.
ISBN 10:1-58685-506-9   ISBN 13:978-1-58685-506-2
1. Incentive awards—United States. 2. Employee motivation—United States. 3. Employee retention—United States. I. Elton, Chester. II. Title.
HF5549.5.I5G6923 2004
658.3'14—dc22

2004008167

About the Authors

Adrian Gostick and Chester Elton are the world's leading authorities on employee motivation. They provide dynamic, humorous and powerful presentations on the power of recognition. Find out more at carrotbooks.com.

Adrian Gostick is coauthor of the UPI International Bestseller *The Integrity Advantage.* An award-winning business author, Adrian also co-wrote the critically acclaimed business book *The 24-Carrot Manager,* called a "must read for modern day managers" by Larry King of CNN. He has written for *USA Today Magazine, Investor's Business Daily* and other national publications, and has been featured on CNBC, MSNBC and National Public Radio. Adrian is director of corporate communication with the O. C. Tanner Company, the world's leading employee-recognition firm. He has a master's degree in strategic communication and leadership from Seton Hall University and is a guest lecturer on organizational culture at that university.

adrian@carrotbooks.com

Chester Elton is coauthor of the best-selling *Managing with Carrots,* nominated as the Society for Human Resource Management (SHRM) Book of the Year. He is also coauthor of *The 24-Carrot Manager.* As a motivation expert, Chester has been interviewed by the *Wall Street Journal* and has been a guest on CNN, Bloomberg Television and on National Public Radio. A sought-after speaker and recognition consultant, Chester is vice president of performance recognition with the O.C. Tanner Recognition Company. He has been a featured speaker at the SHRM annual conference, HR Southwest, *Incentive Magazine* Forums, New York City Premium and Incentive Show, and Chicago Motivation Show. He serves as a recognition consultant to Fortune 100 firms.

chester@carrotbooks.com

Eh, What's Up, Doc?

"Carrots are good for you, Billy. They help you see better." Everyone's mother said that in an effort to get their children to eat more carrots.

And she was right. Carrots are good for you.

Fast forward thirty years, and carrots still play a major role in your health — or, should I say, your career health and your business health.

Now instead of encouraging you to eat carrots, they're dangled for you to grasp. Dangled just out of reach — just enough to "go for it!" Or better, they are offered as a reward for a job well done.

Managers and employers are constantly looking for the secret of "motivating their people." Therein lies the problem. You can't motivate people — BUT you can set an example and create an environment where they will motivate themselves. And you can use "Carrot Power" to make this magic happen.

You can inspire them with carrots.

You can challenge them with carrots.

You can encourage them with carrots.

You can reward their efforts with carrots.

And you can celebrate their achievement with carrots.

As a leader, the secret to creating a successful work environment is to first create an atmosphere in which success can occur. This means a continuous positive attitude on your part, and continuous positive reinforcement for your employees. It means recognizing and rewarding great performance.

The tone for the company is set by creating the right work environment (and the right boss environment). Word of mouth is just as powerful from your employees as it is from your customers. If you treat your customers great and your employees lousy, that mixed message is devastating at the cash register.

So many leaders fail to realize that their employees go home and talk about their day with you, just like customers go home and talk about their purchases and experiences with you. And the internal customer is just as powerful as the external one. When you have a great, productive, high earning team the word gets out. The "law of attraction" kicks in. Great talent will call and want to work for you. What a great dilemma to have.

What you're about to read are 365 ways to turn carrots into gold. Gold for recognition, gold for reward, gold for customer service, gold for internal customer service, gold for productivity, gold for morale, gold for employee retention, gold for customer retention, and gold for corporate profit.

Sure, an apple a day keeps the doctor away. But a carrot a day is positive reinforcement for tasks and projects being completed, customers being served. People are being recognized for a job well done, and happiness reigns supreme.

I challenge you to put Carrot Power to work for you and your company. The golden answers you seek to implement this program are within these pages, skillfully written by recognition experts Gostick and Elton. Read them. Study them. Implement them.

— Jeffrey Gitomer, author of *The Sales Bible* and
Customer Satisfaction is Worthless, Customer Loyalty is Priceless

Introduction

A few years ago, researchers with more funding than sense conducted a survey of 10,000 people. They asked whether the person on the other end of the phone knew how to ride a bike.

Remarkably, out of a sample the size of a major Iowa town, only three people couldn't ride. Thus, we can assume, it's an experience we've all had.

How did we learn to ride our bikes? Whether we grew up in the suburbs, the urban jungle, or a real jungle, some trusted person (Mom or Dad for many of us) trudged out to the road with us. Terrified, we climbed on the bike, pedaled for a few unsteady feet, then fell off. But bless their hearts, those "trusty companions" didn't give up. They steadied us by holding the back of our seats. At great personal discomfort, they ran alongside. And they kept praising our efforts.

"You got a little farther that time."
"Way to go, honey, you've almost got it."
"Hey, I bet that won't even need stitches."

In the end, all the praising and support finally bolstered our courage and we were ready to go it alone. Suddenly, we were riding. Without training wheels. Without anyone's hand guiding us.

Thus, we earned the reward: we were able to ride anywhere on the block on our own.

Yes, we were free. We *owned* the road.

You didn't know it at the time, but you learned your first management lesson that day. It's a lesson that will make you a much more effective leader if you live it. The lesson is this: Great managers—

Praise Effort. Reward Results.

In other words, they use employee recognition — or carrots, as we like to call it — to motivate their work force.

Employees fed a steady diet of carrots focus better on company goals. They spot new opportunities faster. They have longer employment life spans (translation: lower turnover). And they can lift companies higher than you might have dreamed possible.

Yet for something that seems so straightforward, it's amazing how many managers get it wrong. We could fill a Central American soccer stadium with leaders who don't believe they need to offer any praise or rewards. These are the guys who offer such thoughtful contributions to leadership as:

"They get their recognition every two weeks in their paycheck."

"I don't care if they like me, as long as they respect me."

"If they want warm and fuzzy, they can buy a puppy."

We've also met a gaggle of managers who sincerely want to reward their people but just seem to get it wrong. They end up offering tangible rewards, but not for tangible results. These are the well-meaning but misguided leaders who offer rewards for effort alone.

"We didn't quite hit our goals this quarter, but I'm going to go ahead and give you the reward anyway. After all, you worked really, really hard."

And finally, there are the lazy cheapskates who, after their people do great things, offer at best only token verbal praise for those real results.

> *"Yep, we landed the big contract. Way to go everyone. Now let's get back to work."*

If an apple a day can keep the doctor away, then *A Carrot A Day* can keep *you* away from recognition pitfalls and help you develop employees who are more focused, more committed and more engaged in your noble cause.

In this book, we offer you 365 easy-to-use recognition ideas, hints and pieces of advice. Read one a day and you will become a better leader — a manager who is able to tap the power of recognition to build a stronger workplace where people come, stay and are committed to your goals.

JANUARY

*Recognition must be
focused on the right behaviors.*

TELL THEM WHAT IS IMPORTANT

Your employees want to make you happy. They really do want to do those things that matter most to you. But chances are, they don't know what specific actions you value. As you begin to recognize your employees, determine what is most important in your department and choose those values that you will recognize.

Many managers identify things such as:

- Customer service
- Integrity
- Innovation
- Leadership
- Ownership

- On-time delivery
- Quality
- Teamwork
- Respect for the individual
- Fun (yes, really, it's okay)

Take some time today to identify your department's key values. Then use those values as the foundation of your recognition efforts.

"If businesses are to grow their way out of the current economic malaise, they will have to get more productivity out of their people — not by cutting and slashing, but by nurturing, engaging and recognizing."

— *John A. Byrne, editor-in-chief,* Fast Company *magazine*

PLAYING IT SMART IN TOUGH ECONOMIES

In a down economy, a manager's first instinct is to cut back. And the "soft side" of business — including recognition programs — is often the first to be slashed.

But when you cut recognition, you are sacrificing the future.

Recognition is the lifeblood of innovation, retention and productivity. It's what keeps employees motivated in the tough times. (And it's why they'll still be devoted when things improve.)

That's why more and more companies are choosing to step up recognition in the tough times, rather than stepping away from it.

REMEMBER: Keeping recognition doesn't mean you're "going soft."

It means you're playing it smart.

Employees don't leave jobs.
They leave managers.

MANAGING FOR *KEEPS*

Many managers we talk with say it's the job of senior management or human resources to make employees feel good about their jobs. That's ironic, since employees overwhelmingly tell us that it should come from *you.*

You observe their work ethic. You write their performance appraisals. You're there when they succeed or fail. You know their names and faces.

Research shows that people see praise as much more sincere from someone they work with every day than from a senior leader they may see a couple of times a month.

When it comes to recognition, the buck stops *here.*

In sales, she really cleaned up.
In appreciation, why not ...

GET HER THINGS IN ORDER

Time. We never seem to have enough. Create some free moments for a top employee by hiring a three-hour maid service for her.

Let them straighten up her place, while she cleans up the marketplace for you.

*Reserved parking spaces
make a great reward.*

TRADING SPACES

If you park near your building and some of your employees park near the equator, trade parking spots for a week as recognition of a job well done. This small act of kindness will go a long way . . . literally. And, the walk will do you good.

"The celebration of one success launches a thousand more."

— Adrian Gostick and Chester Elton, authors

SET SAIL

You might think recognition is centered in the past. But it's really all about the future.

People repeat behaviors that are recognized. Public recognition motivates everyone in the room to do more of what spawned the award. In this way, recognition becomes a catalyst for increasingly on-track, above-and-beyond performance.

Don't pick the wrong carrot.

GETTING AWARDS RIGHT

To have the intended effect, a reward's value should be an appropriate symbol of the employee's effort and its outcome. After all, we all know that winning a million-dollar contract deserves more than a T-shirt or key chain, right?

Apparently not.

When she was first out of college, recognition consultant Kathe Farris began working for a bank. She started near the bottom of the corporate ladder, answering phones. During a promotion to cross-sell mutual funds, she was able to bring a whopping $1.2 million into the bank.

"So what did they give me?" asks Kathe. She scoffs at her own answer. "A mug." Kathe shakes her head incredulously: "A mug," she repeats. "Do you think I — or anyone else who worked around me — ever sold mutual funds again? Of course not."

When choosing an award, be aware of its symbolic value. In some cases, a mug is appropriate. In others, it is absolutely not.

REMEMBER: There are a lot of onions out there masquerading as carrots. And a thoughtless award can leave a bad taste in an employee's mouth.

"I can't get no . . . satisfaction."

— *Mick Jagger, musician*

SATISFACTION GUARANTEED

In the side yard of one of our childhood homes, there was a section of lawn that constantly sunk. Quite often, my father would spend a Saturday filling in the sinkhole with dirt.

For a while, it would seem to work. But gradually we would notice a slight depression. Try as we might, we could not fill the increasing void. As a child, it was fascinating — and a little bit terrifying.

In our travels, we've seen managers with the same fear in their eyes. Desperate to satiate the sinking morale around them, they offer money, perks, benefits. Nothing works.

Except recognition.

Today, take a look at who works with you. When was the last time they received positive recognition from you? If it has been a while, change that today.

Reading between the lines.

AUTHOR! AUTHOR!

Sometimes it's best to play things by the book.

If you notice one of your employees reading on her lunch hour or talking about a favorite novel, remember that a new release from that author might be a wonderful, thoughtful reward for above-and-beyond behavior.

Praise and recognition must be frequent.

EVERY SEVEN DAYS

Research shows that committed employees receive praise and recognition from their immediate supervisor at least once every seven days.

We hear from a lot of supervisors who worry that the activity of praising will lose meaning. In return, we'll ask: "How often do you tell your wife you love her (your husband you love him)?" They usually answer, "Probably every day."

We then ask, "What would happen if instead of every day, you just said it once or twice a year. Maybe on their birthday and your anniversary. Would that cut it?"

"Are you kidding?"

"Why not?"

"Because she (he) wants to hear it." And before the words are out of the managers' mouths, the light goes on.

As employees, most of us can never receive enough sincere recognition. It never gets old.

He's given the performance of a lifetime.

SEND HIM TO THE BIG SHOW

If one of your above-and-beyond employees deserves recognition, think about rewarding him with a couple of tickets to a concert or ball game he's been eager to see.

Then take note of how quickly he finds his way back to the spotlight again.

Give an award that really goes the distance.

A HOLE IN ONE

If you have a budding sportsman on your staff, a thoughtful carrot might be an hour or two of golf lessons — and time off to enjoy them!

*"We're totally dependent on the ideas and talent
of our people, so we have to help them
feel great about themselves."*

— *Bob Jeffrey, North America division president, J. Walter Thompson*

WHAT GOES AROUND, COMES AROUND

When employees look good, so do you. When they succeed, you do too. So, go ahead, do *yourself* a favor and make *them* feel marvelous!

People who feel good, work good. Okay, we know it's bad grammar, but it's good sense.

Recognize their family.

SEND THANKS HOME

We were in Michigan one gray winter day, speaking to a great automotive supply company. At one point, the vice president of HR told us she recognizes the families of employees.

For example, she said, "Recently I had an employee who had to work late for several weeks straight to put in a new software system. It was hard work, and I appreciated his great effort. At the end of the period, on a Friday afternoon, I sent his wife flowers and a note of thanks."

When the employee showed up for work on Monday morning, she asked, "So, did your wife get the flowers?" He nodded. "Yep. Now she wants me to work harder for you."

Talk about motivation! Recognizing families or partners for their sacrifices is undoubtedly one of the most powerful (and yet untapped) motivational tools we have ever seen.

It's an idea that passes the smell test.

Carrots improve your eyesight.

RECOGNITION BY WALKING AROUND

They say carrots improve your eyesight. And it's true. Spend part of every day walking, or driving, if necessary, through your work locations talking to your people. Notice what they are doing. Ask them about their assignments.

In a notebook, make notes for potential recognition stories as you walk around. These day-to-day stories are the ones that will add spice to your recognition ceremonies and informal recognition moments.

See what we're talking about?

> *"One of the greatest challenges of businesses today is creating a culture that is both values-centered and performance-driven. Many business executives believe they must make trade-offs between the two. I don't buy it."*
>
> — *Bill George, retired CEO, Medtronic*

GETTING IT STRAIGHT

Every now and then, our kids will announce that it is backwards day. Speech, clothes, hair, walking — it's all backwards. We remember playing that game, too, as kids. Ironically, some leaders in corporate America are still all turned around.

We're sure some leader (in a helpful sort of way) has told you before that you must abdicate either your values or your performance standard. You can't have it both ways.

Sadly, they've got it all backwards. Corporate values are intricately intertwined with performance. One directly impacts the other.

Here's how it really works for the most successful companies: Recognition sharpens employee focus on company values and goals, allowing your work force to get more of the most important things done — and directly boosting performance.

And that's the truth. Pure and simple.

Stop! And . . .

HUDDLE UP!

At one great grocery store chain in the heartland, employees *and* customers are encouraged to "huddle up" for recognition moments. Everything in the store stops for a few moments to recognize a great associate.

What a great — and almost unheard of — idea. Simply <u>stop.</u> Stop chasing. Stop calling. Stop meeting. Stop worrying. Today, take a moment to stop what you are doing, call your people together, and give someone a much-deserved pat on the back.

It promises to be the start of something good.

Some stories just have to be shared.

GET IT IN WRITING

Imagine an issue of your company newsletter featuring an achievement by one of your employees. Now imagine it yellow and worn with age. (We just thought you might want to see how it will look years from now in your employee's scrapbook.)

Your company newsletter is the ideal place to recognize outstanding employees. Submit employees' names and photographs to the newsletter with a story about what they have done to live the corporate values. Don't worry about spelling or punctuation; just tell the story. If they are smart, the editors will take your story and take care of the details.

Your employee will save that article for years. Guaranteed. And each time he sees it, he'll feel the desire to be in the spotlight again.

It's never too early to start thinking about recognition.

THE MILLION-DOLLAR QUESTION

When you are hiring a new employee, ask the person to share her most memorable recognition moment — when she was honored for above-and-beyond behavior. Ask what she did to earn the reward, what she was given, and how it made her feel.

Not only is this a great way to uncover an applicant's strengths, it also can give you an idea of what types of rewards will be valued by this person in the future.

"Life isn't a matter of milestones but of moments."

— *Rose Kennedy, mother of U.S. President John F. Kennedy*

MINUTE-BY-MINUTE RECOGNITION

Less than sixty seconds. That's all it takes to make someone's day, using on-the-spot recognition. The next time you notice an employee doing something right, immediately follow these four simple steps:

1) Tell them exactly what they did that was right ("Wanda, I noticed that you picked up the phones today, since Bess was sick.")

2) Tell them what value or goal they met. ("That shows a lot of teamwork.")

3) Explain how that impacts the company. ("We might have missed that emergency call from our biggest customer without your help.")

4) Express appreciation. ("Thanks so much.")

NOTE: In less time than it took you to read this page, you could have recognized someone. Now, how easy is that!

Employees need to know you care about them as individuals.

GET TO KNOW 'EM

When you hire a new employee, ask, "If you had a day off to spend as you wanted, what you would do and where you would go?" You'll learn a lot about the employee in those few minutes. Maybe the employee likes fishing (half a day off might be a great reward), the arts (tickets to the symphony), sports (tickets to a game) or reading (a new release on a favorite topic).

Make a note of your employee's interests and then use those interests to determine what day-to-day rewards you can offer. Not only will this give you great ideas for recognition, it will show that you have interest in them as a person.

"Too often we underestimate the power of a touch,
a smile, a kind word, a listening ear, an honest compliment,
or the smallest act of caring,
all of which have the potential to turn a life around."

— *Leo Buscaglia, author and lecturer*

THE LITTLE THINGS REALLY *DO* MATTER MOST

We know a guy who keeps a few short notes from his wife in his wallet. Sweet nothings, really. He tells us that sometimes, when searching for a membership or business card, he'll stumble upon them.

"Or, on a really bad day at the office, I might purposely dig them out," he says.

No matter the occasion, reading them always puts him back on top of the world. A little thing, yes. But what an amazing impact!

The same thing goes for recognition at the office. It doesn't have to be big, flashy, or expensive. A hand-written thank-you note, or a few words of praise in front of an employee's peers at staff meeting. These small things can mean the world to employees. And the simple memory of that recognition might be just what is needed to push an employee's performance over the top.

On second thought, this may not be so little after all.

The Dirty Dozen of Why We Don't

EXCUSE NO. 1

"I DON'T HAVE THE TIME!"

What did your mother always tell you? You make time to do the things you want to do. If it is important, you will find the time to do it. If you want to inspire someone and show real appreciation, you will find the time. (And, when you think about it, how much time do you need to write a thank-you note or say "thanks!" Not much!)

Be interested in their families.

CARROTS FOR KIDS

You do something nice for me, I appreciate it. You do something nice for my family, and all of a sudden *we* are family.

Today, before you leave the office, ask each of your employees about their kids. Find out when their birthdays are and how old each child is. On your calendar, mark those dates and celebrate with them — whether through a small gift or even a simple birthday card with a hand-written note. A thoughtful picture book or toy given on the birthday of your employee's five-year-old daughter could be the best thing you've ever done for morale and will certainly bring you closer to your employee.

Is it important to be close with your employees? Let us put it this way: do you work harder for people you like and who like you, or those who seem aloof and superior?

Have some fun with it.

WASH AWAY YOUR TROUBLES

Recognition doesn't need to be stuffy and formal. One company we visited had a car wash to celebrate record earnings. Senior management grabbed buckets and rags and washed every car in the parking lot to thank employees for their great work.

Who wouldn't want to say to the CEO, "Hey, buddy, you missed a spot."

Don't be afraid to reward achievers.

RECOGNIZE ONE PERSON EVERY WEEK

When planning recognition, some managers worry about offending an employee or leaving someone out. So they opt to "recognize everyone" as a group. These managers not only end up alienating the stars that make a difference but *reinforcing* the behavior of their average and poor performers.

Instead of serving up mass praise to your work group, try this: put together a chart of all your people and recognize one person in each weekly staff meeting until you have publicly recognized them all. Don't just recognize for "overall greatness," but for specific behaviors that are important to you and your organization.

When you start recognizing people, you'll be amazed at how easy it is and how nobody feels left out. You'll also find yourself recognizing faster (even on the spot) for the "right" behaviors. In most cases, you'll also notice your employees recognizing each other and vying for more of your recognition.

"It is not an accident that the best places to work are also the places that make the most money."

— *Gordon Bethune, chairman, Continental Airlines*

SHARING THE WEALTH

At this airline, besides company parties, profit sharing and employee recognition, Continental has a program where employees with perfect attendance are entered in a raffle to win a new Ford Explorer.

(Talk about *driving* performance forward!)

Sometimes the best reward is time with the boss.

FACE TIME WITH THE BIG CHEESE

For many employees, the best reward is knowing their actions are being noticed — by you *and* by others in senior positions.

Consider rewarding a great employee by taking her along on your next meeting with senior management. Speak about the projects the employee is working on and her contributions to your team's success.

You'll not only garner loyalty from your employee but you'll be seen as a nurturing team player by your bosses.

A tune-up could make your employee-recognition program purr.
(Not to mention your employees.)

VROOM! VROOM!

Is it time to rework your employee recognition system? Then you'll appreciate this tool.

In 1964, researcher Victor Vroom proposed that employees are motivated to work toward rewards that (1) they want and (2) they believe they have a realistic chance of obtaining. Based on this "Expectancy Theory," Vroom suggested that when designing reward systems leaders should:

- Make a clear connection between performance and outcome.

- Develop flexible reward systems that provide a variety of potentially attractive outcomes.

- Determine what rewards the employee values.

- Ensure that employees receive appropriate training and have the ability to perform the job successfully.

Take a few moments to evaluate how well your current recognition program meets these criteria. A few critical adjustments could have employee performance going from zero to incredible in no time at all.

Play hooky from work . . . together.

TAKE IN A SHOW

As a team reward, take everyone to an inspirational movie (anything with Denzel might do) on a Friday afternoon and then send them home early. Throw in some popcorn and licorice.

Playing hooky is always easier when the boss is along for the ride.

> *"Attention, employers:*
> *Make sure your employees feel valued.*
> *Otherwise, they could bolt for other jobs*
> *as soon as the economy starts to improve."*

— *Jane Kim,* Wall Street Journal

DON'T TAKE THEM FOR GRANTED

The news is less than earth-shaking, we know: how you treat employees during a down economy seriously impacts how they will treat your company when it rebounds.

Sure, it's not surprising, but it is something to think about, given the recent revelation by the *Wall Street Journal* that 40 percent of workers have strong negative feelings about their jobs.

Plan for the future today by reenergizing your employee-recognition program. You'll be glad you did.

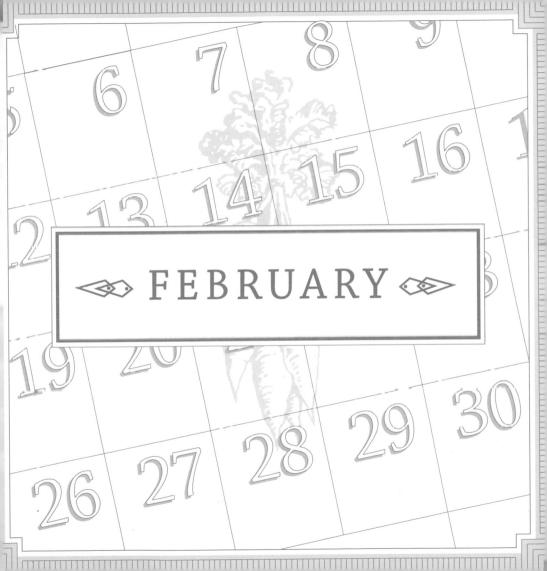

FEBRUARY

Point employee efforts in the right direction.

REINFORCE THE CREDO

Does your organization have a formal credo, vision or values statement? Do all your employees know what that statement is and what it means to your department? If they don't, talk about the statement in your next recognition celebration.

For example, "I wanted to gather to recognize Julie today. One of the values we really believe around here is teamwork. And nobody epitomizes that better than Julie. Just last month, I was complaining about not being able to get the information we needed from accounting. So Julie set up weekly meetings with our contact over there. I know I speak for all of us when I say things are vastly improved now, due to Julie's teamwork."

Recognition ceremonies are communication opportunities, perfect times to reinforce what is most important to you and your organization.

Recognition can happen, even if you're miles away.

ONE A DAY WHEN YOU'RE OUT

When you travel, there are most likely people who fill in for you — an assistant, a staff member, a colleague. One supervisor we talked with at a manufacturing company found a way to thank his only employee when he was on the road.

"I had a staff of six a few years ago. Now, with the declining economy, there are only two of us left. So, it's more important than ever to recognize," he said. "With my employee, I understand her as an individual. For example, a simple thing, but she loves chocolate chip cookies."

So when the supervisor went on a week-long business trip, he left her $3 — enough to buy a fresh-baked cookie from the cafeteria each day. Said the manager, "She's stuck in the office, picking up the slack while I'm traveling, so I want to make sure that every day some recognition is happening."

Don't forget to smile.

A GRIN AN HOUR

This may sound a bit ridiculous, but next time you glance in the mirror, try out your smile. The more you smile and laugh, the more your employees will, too. Come on, grouchy-pants, it's not so tough. We all like to be around fun people, and your employees will like you a lot more if you are smiling and laughing instead of grimacing and frowning.

Attitude matters — and it's contagious. Just like a yawn will trigger others to follow suit, smiles make people smile. Start a trend at work, a trend of happy people.

"Incentives are the only way to make people work harder."

— *Nikita Kruschev, former premier of the Soviet Union*

"CAPITALIZE" ON EMPLOYEES' DESIRE TO ACHIEVE

So, if Kruschev knew this, why didn't communism fall sooner in the former Soviet Union? Hmmm. Maybe he needed an incentive to push him towards change.

The same goes for you. If you've been procrastinating your own revolution toward recognition, make yourself an offer you can't refuse. If you'd love a massage, schedule one immediately after you do an awards presentation. You'll feel better — and so will your staff.

Rally your people to the cause.

ASSIGN CONFIDENCE

It's a timeworn tradition: Before the battle, before the big game, a leader steps forward to rally the troops.

There's a reason for that: it works. When people believe in themselves — and know someone else does, too, — it's amazing what they can accomplish.

Try this next time you assign a new task to a person or team: State out loud that you are sure the assignment can be completed. Then express your confidence in the person or team who is taking on the assignment.

Be sincere. It's important that you believe what you are saying. And remember, it's ultimately your responsibility to help your team members achieve what you have assigned them by providing resources and direction, if needed.

This could be a red-letter day.

FROM THE OFFICE OF THE PRESIDENT

Have your company president write a letter of thanks to an employee who has put forth his very best effort and then some. It's one letter that, most likely, will be kept forever.

"It is not how much we give but what we put into the giving."

— *Mother Teresa, Nobel Peace Prize winner*

PUT YOUR HEART INTO IT

Sometimes it's not so much what we say but how we say it. A sincere thank-you doesn't come from a well-written script but from a sincere heart. Don't worry that the words aren't elegant; just make sure the feeling is right.

Take recognition to the next level.

TELL YOUR BOSS

Send a voice mail or e-mail to your boss, praising a great employee. (Don't forget to cc the employee.)

*"The more you praise and celebrate your life,
the more there is in life to celebrate."*

— *Oprah Winfrey, celebrity*

CELEBRATE LIFE

Celebrating achievements isn't just a job — it's a way of life. As we learn to look for things to celebrate at work, we'll begin to find them at home and school, in our churches and neighborhoods. We will find ourselves enjoying the moment and developing the same grateful, gracious attitude we've so often admired in others.

Miraculously, we find that in seeking to enrich the lives of those around us through celebrations, we have truly enriched our own.

Start new hires off on a good note.

SING THEIR PRAISES

New-employee orientation is the best time, most experts agree, to begin the formal-recognition process. A small award during the first few weeks on the job helps bond a new hire to an organization — and to you, their boss — and helps retain the employee during the stressful training period.

On one survey, 90 percent of people were able to recite their date of hire and the details of their first day on the job. As a boss, you only get one chance at that first day. Make it count! If do you it right, there will be lots of positive days to follow.

"That rabbit's plum loco!"

— *Yosemite Sam, cartoon character*

REWARD FAILURE

Make a person feel good about making a mistake based on the risk they took with good intentions.

People are afraid to risk in their jobs, primarily because of fear that failure will bring some sort of reprisal or ridicule. When this atmosphere is present, growth and innovation are stunted.

Several years ago, I began giving reward to employees for mistakes. The results were astounding. I found that people were so surprised and emotionally relieved, that many times they actually cried when I gave them the reward. I realized that people didn't make mistakes on purpose, and that many times the mistakes were in an effort to succeed, or simply trying to navigate uncharted waters.

"It's gotten so that now an employee, fresh from a major screw-up, will sheepishly enter my office and say, 'I think I need a bonus.'"

— *submitted by Jeffrey Gitomer, author of* The Sales Bible *and* Customer Satisfaction is Worthless, Customer Loyalty is Priceless

Watching an award presentation, coworkers can't help but wonder ...

WHAT WOULD THEY SAY ABOUT ME?

It's happened to us. Probably to you, too. As you watch an award presentation, you find yourself thinking, "What would they have said about me?" And deep down inside, you know you'd really like to find out.

That's the power of recognition. It affects everyone in attendance, not just the employee in the spotlight. It gets them thinking and planning. One thing is sure: no one tunes out during a recognition moment.

That's exactly why it's the perfect place to talk about your company values. By recognizing very specific employee achievements and showing how they support company goals, you teach employees to think strategically — minus the long, boring speeches. Everything you say during an award presentation is couched in a very personal, emotionally charged context that goes straight to employees' hearts (where a wallet card or newsletter could never go). And the award itself provides the motivation for employees to go out and get it done.

"I like it, I love it, I want some more of it!"

— Tim McGraw, country music star

FEED THE ADDICTION

Recognition is like potato chips. Bet you can't stop at just one. In fact, recognition can be so addicting, at times we've wondered if it should come with a warning from the surgeon general. (Warning: Recognition can be extremely beneficial to your organization's health. You may not be able to make yourself quit.)

But, then, why would you want to?

Recognition builds confidence. It fans the fire of achievement, and gives people the courage to try. ("After all, I did it once. Why not again?")

You've felt it before. When we are complimented for our efforts and good work, we gain momentum. We gain the power to overcome obstacles and problems because we know people support and believe in us.

*"Take the time today to send flowers and a card
to someone you love."*

— *FTD*

THIS TIME, WITH FEELING

Yes, it's a commercial, but what a great point.

Business aside, when is the last time you recognized the most important people in your life?

Don't miss this chance to tell the people closest to you that you love them. No one can hear it enough and it never gets old. It will make whoever gets the roses feel great — and you won't feel so bad yourself.

Management Etiquette Rule No. 1:

CALL EMPLOYEES BY NAME

This is a case when name-calling is actually good.

Use employees' names whenever possible — when you recognize them, when you praise them, even when you greet them in the morning. Calling people by name is one of the most basic forms of recognition. It shows you recognize them not only as employees but as individuals.

And no, "Hey good looking," just doesn't qualify. And "Nice work, Sparky" is completely out.

Lights! Camera! Recognition!

GIVE EMPLOYEES A STARRING ROLE

Give your star performer the star treatment by using him in a training film, internal video or commercial. When the project is finished, award him his own copy, along with a thank-you note. He'll love it . . . if you can just coax him out of his trailer.

The Dirty Dozen of Why We Don't

EXCUSE NO. 2

"IT WILL LOSE ITS IMPACT IF I DO TOO MUCH!"

Yeah, and if you cross your eyes too long, they'll stay that way. When was the last time anyone at work said, "Man, this place gives too much recognition!" Our guess is, let's see . . . NEVER!

And by the way, it doesn't ever get old if you really mean it. Does anyone ever tire of someone saying you matter and you are important? So don't worry; just keep doing it.

Don't underestimate the value of applause.

OVATIONS WILL MOVE YOU

Do you remember the times in your life when you were applauded? Most of us do.

At one fast-food chain, if an employee is working hard and feeling a little overwhelmed or under-appreciated, she can ask for a standing ovation at any time. Everyone in the restaurant — including customers — gives the person applause.

Gather your employees now and then for a standing ovation of one of your people. Explain the great things the person has done, and then start the applause. Dabbing the corners of teary eyes is optional.

Let them know you were thinking of them.

BRING THEM SOMETHING BACK

When traveling on a business trip, bring something back for your staff to enjoy. It doesn't have to be expensive. This is one case where it really is the thought that counts. Bring home a case of apples from Washington or chocolate from Europe. This is really easy if you're attending a convention. Just pick up a few extra-cool giveaways like T-shirts, squeezy toys or blinking ballpoint pens to share with the folks back home.

You'll find that, in this case at least, absence really does make the heart grow fonder.

To get recognition right, you must have ...

PERFECT TIMING

Informal rewards — everything from hand-written cards to movie tickets, from spa trips to a free lunch — should typically be presented at least once a month to the people who create the most value and at least once a quarter to your core performers.

"If you just set out to be liked,
you would be prepared to compromise on anything at any time,
and you would achieve nothing."

— *Margaret Thatcher, former British prime minister*

HAVE YOU GOT IT FIGURED OUT?

Giving praise without a purpose is like a boat with holes in it. It just doesn't float.

Recognition is not about being nice; it's about results. So, before you make a single award presentation, sit down and figure out what you want to accomplish. Don't hold back; imagine your ideal future. Then consider these specifics:

- What do our clients value?
- What does the company value?
- What do our employees value?
- What is our basic purpose?
- What is our competitive situation?
- What will make us more productive, more valuable to our company, more efficient in the purpose of our vision?

Once you've got a plan, put it into action through recognition.

*Employees can write the book
on procedures. Let them!*

TAKE NOTE OF WHAT EMPLOYEES HAVE TO SAY

Here's a great way to show employees that you are listening: interview your staff and capture their wisdom about "how we get things done around here" on paper. Put the thoughts together in an organized manner and hand it out to new hires when they start.

Your new people will benefit from the accumulated knowledge, and your established employees will feel honored that you think that much of their opinions.

This reward really hits the spot.

STRESS-REDUCING RECOGNITION

For a team reward, bring in a massage therapist and chair for a day. Your employees will not only thank you, they'll be healthier. It'll be a day they will remember and work hard to make happen again.

Ahhhh.

This award program will get their hearts racing.

FLEX YOUR RECOGNITION MUSCLES

Set goals for individuals to get fit. Reward employees who exercise a certain number of days in a month. Give healthy rewards, like fruit baskets or exercise equipment.

The need for appreciation is timeless.

SOME THINGS NEVER CHANGE

In a 1949 study, employees were asked to rank the rewards of their jobs. Then their managers were asked to rank what they believed the employees wanted. Highest on the employees' lists were (1) feeling appreciated and 2) feeling that they were being informed about things that were happening. Managers were blown away. They had believed their employees would put good wages and job security first.

In fact, most managers had no idea how highly their employees valued appreciation.

The study was repeated in the 1980s and again recently. The result? Each time, the findings were exactly the same.

Recognition makes it hard for employees to leave.

FORGET THE GOLDEN HANDCUFFS

Carrots — in the form of rewards and recognition — make it hard for employees to pull up roots and move to another company. Face it, most people can give up a corner office with a window without a lot of heartburn. They won't bat an eye while swapping one benefits plan for another. They'll even sacrifice a company car or a nice office. But they won't part with appreciation and rewards.

There are very real costs associated with leaving a job, and the more social ties that exist, the greater those costs will be. Appreciation captures the heart and the mind. Don't miss the chance to lock up a great employee with recognition.

> *"You can have everything in life you want, if you will just help enough other people get what they want."*
>
> — *Zig Ziglar, motivational speaker*

YOU GET BACK WHAT YOU GIVE

Some people approach work like an after-Christmas sale: hogging (the good assignments), grabbing (the spotlight) and hoarding (praise and rewards). These poor folks have it all backwards.

Discounting others only brings you down too. On the other hand, help your employees with their goals and they will walk through fire to accomplish yours.

Take some time today to review employee goals with them and come up with concrete ways to help make them reality. Then see if you notice a difference next time you give them an assignment.

Get ideas. Get support. Get signed up.

JOIN THE CLUB

No one knows all the answers. But savvy leaders know where to get them. To garner the latest and greatest data and ideas about recognition, join an association, attend a recognition conference or subscribe to a magazine that focuses on just that.

Do it, and you'll thank us later.

MARCH

> **"To better the lives of others
> is one of your life's greatest rewards."**
>
> — *Captain Len Kaine, president, Golden Rule Society*

BUILD. DON'T TEAR DOWN

If you had to list five things that are going wrong in your office right now, what would they be? Now, how about five things that are right on track? Stumped?

It's always easier to find fault than to build up. Master builders devote years to structures that can be destroyed in minutes by vandals and looters. Your people are much the same.

When you honor someone's contributions in front of their peers in a dignified way, you build people. When you criticize them in front of their peers, you destroy them.

Use recognition liberally and your criticism sparingly. Trust and confidence are built over time and with great care. Recognition moments can help you build solid and valuable relationships.

Take care to reserve sharp comments and criticism for one-on-one meetings. Recognition is public; criticism is private.

It's your job to get them there.

PUTTING EMPLOYEES IN THE LEAD

Most senior leaders know that one of the measures of a great manager is how many leaders that person has developed. If you haven't developed many leaders, it's time to start.

To become future leaders, your employees must be empowered, and they need your support and confidence. Then, when they act in a way that demonstrates leadership, they need you to recognize their behavior.

A free lunch is good.
Her favorite people make it great.

LET HER CREATE THE GUEST LIST

As a reward, take an employee to lunch and let her bring three or four of her favorite coworkers. Make the event fun, and let everyone in attendance know that lunch is not about you, but about the person you are honoring.

They say the early bird gets the worm.

MEET AND GREET

You snooze, you lose ... a prime opportunity for recognition.

Get employees energized first thing in the morning by greeting them at the door and telling them you are glad they are at work. Double the impact by having the coffee brewing and providing donuts or bagels.

Start the day off right, and chances are it will go better all day long.

Don't let your praise get too sketchy.

DETAILS MATTER

The next time your young child, grandchild or niece brings home a Rorschach painting from school, try an experiment. Instead of patting her on the head and saying, "Aren't you just the best little artist," try talking to your child about the specifics of the painting.

"Why did you use red here?" "What have you drawn here?" "What action is going on in this area?"

And then, when you praise the child and hang the painting on the refrigerator, use specifics, such as "I love how your flowers are turning toward the sun; that's very observant," or "You know, I don't know that I've ever seen scarier blue alien bugs." We guarantee that your little one will light up to such specific praise and remember it for a much longer time.

Of course, these principles apply at work. Be specific about your employees' achievements and they will be thrilled.

"Put your appreciation into action by taking time
to show your appreciation.
Tell one or more people something you appreciate about them.
Remember, what you put out comes back."

— *Doc Childre and Sara Paddison, HeartMath Discovery Program*

GET IT BY GIVING

We often find that the managers who most strongly resist recognition programs are those who have rarely (or never) been recognized themselves. If they could only once experience the taste of a carrot, it would change their minds. If they could feel the emotion and see the good it does for them, it would be easier for them to give that feeling to someone else.

In your corporation, are there any managers who could use a carrot? If so, be the one in your workplace to activate the power of recognition and appreciation in their lives.

Remember, recognition has to start somewhere. Why not with you?

"There is always a better way."

— *Thomas Edison, inventor*

REWARD INNOVATION

Constantly be on the lookout for people doing simple things better. Those are the people who, bit by bit, make your organization successful. Be on the lookout for ways to recognize them.

Take the time to recognize their innovative efforts, and sure as shootin', there'll be more to come.

Help your employees recognize each other.

GIVE THEM THE TOOLS

Creating a culture of recognition in your work group is often as simple as giving them the tools. Try giving each of your employees a stack of thank-you cards and asking them to please begin to recognize each other when they see a coworker demonstrating company or team values.

There is one caveat: your employees will receive this instruction with a favorable attitude only if you've set the example first. You'll find if you are free with your praise, your employees will quickly get on board.

Never underestimate the power of a thank-you.

To be effective, praise must be specific.

NO MORE "GOOD JOBS"

At one of California's largest theme parks — run by a man-sized rodent — managers are told to avoid generic praise like "Good job." Officials there have discovered that general praise can actually have a negative impact on employees.

It's true. Just imagine that you've been working hard all day, making sure rides are running smoothly, that guests are safe, that people are happy. You are hot. You're hungry. And about fifteen kids in a row have rubbed cotton candy on your uniform. But, hey, you're still smiling.

Then your manager wanders by for the first time that day and fires off a glib, "Hey, Stevie. Keep up the good work." Your response: "That bozo has no idea what I've been doing."

Compare that with a manager who is watching your good work. Perhaps she comments, "Steve, I was really impressed with how you handled the guests at your ride during that break for maintenance. The folks seemed a little put out, but your positive attitude kept them smiling. Thanks so much."

"I have always been a sucker for attention"

— Cuba Gooding Jr., actor

BRING OUT THE STAR INSIDE THEM

Aren't we all WHAT? Don't think so? Just watch the fans standing behind reporters during live news broadcasts. They'll do anything but fly to attract attention.

Like moths to light, people inherently seek their fifteen minutes of fame. (Fortunately, some do it more intelligently than others.) Take the time today to put an employee on a podium and watch what happens. Don't be surprised to see his or her performance take flight.

Remember to thank people who have influenced you.

A CARROT FOR THE TEACHER

We've all had at least one teacher who made a difference in our lives. Perhaps a motivating English teacher, a master of math or a savvy shop instructor left a lasting impact. Send that dedicated educator a handwritten letter of thanks and explain, specifically, how they made a difference to you.

Chances are, your letter will be the best thing that happens to that teacher this week.

A magazine subscription is
a monthly reminder of your regard.

TWELVE MONTHS OF PRAISE

An interesting reward idea is to give your employee a year's subscription to her favorite magazine. Make sure the magazine is in good taste. And just because your business is computer software, don't assume she'll be giddy over *Microchips Illustrated.*

The Dirty Dozen of Why We Don't

EXCUSE NO. 3

"I DON'T HAVE THE BUDGET FOR RECOGNITION"

True! We all wish we had a million dollars. But recognition doesn't have to cost a lot. Remember, it's how you make people feel that is important. A stack of thank-you cards costs pennies. Certificates can be printed for next to nothing on a color printer. An e-mail to the boss or an announcement of achievement costs nothing! Get creative! The more you put into the idea, the more it will mean to those who receive it.

Understand the meaning of recognition.

CARROTS DEFINED

It's important to note that Merriam-Webster defines the root of the word *recognition* as "re," which means "to do again," and *cognition,* which means "to know." Thus, recognition is "to know again."

The first step of effective recognition requires you to know your people well. Ask yourself these questions:

- Are my people in the right positions so they will be self-motivated?
- Do they know what is expected of them?
- Do they have the right tools?
- Do I give them the freedom to do their best work?
- Do I give them praise and recognition to recall and celebrate achievements and milestones?

Tighten your belts — with an exercise program.

BUILD A LEAN, MEAN FIGHTING MACHINE

Research shows that healthy employees are more productive — and that can't help but improve your bottom line (literally). To help get people in shape, sponsor a weight-loss challenge. Reward the person or team that loses the greatest percentage of their body weight with a healthy prize. It's a great way to do more with less.

A HANDCLASP — A SMILE — AND A WORD

By David Horton Elton (Chester's grandfather)

He came in with a "chip on his shoulder,"
  He left with a "smile on his face,"
What was it that changed his demeanor?
  What was it that really took place?
Would you like to know just what happened?
  Would you care to learn what occurred?
It's simple, easy of access:
  "A Handclasp, a Smile and a Word."
A "Handclasp" that made him feel "welcome,"
  Seemed somehow to start things off right,
A "Sit down, and let's talk it over,"
  Vetoed his "spoil" for a fight.

A "smile" countermanding contention,
  Will anger and discord assuage,
A "Let's get together and reason,"
  Represses resentment and rage.
A "word," gently tempered with kindness —
  A patient word, seasoned with tact —
A word, not combative and churlish —
  A truthful word — stating the fact.
So the "tonic" to avoid disagreement —
  Try it out, I'm sure you'll concur —
The best of all "medicines," brother ,
  "A Handclasp, a Smile and a Word."

REMEMBER: When you treat people with respect and dignity,
        you get the best from them.

What motivates top employees?
Hint: it's not green

BREAKING THE BREAD BARRIER

On St. Patrick's Day, it's appropriate to talk about something green. And every employee does have his price for high performance. It's not always paid in currency but in the form of appreciation.

In a 2000 survey of 551 large employers, Watson and Wyatt found that only 15 percent of employees say expectations of financial reward are "very significant" influences on performance. In contrast, 66 percent named appreciation as a very significant motivator.

It seems there really are things that money can't buy. But, fortunately, appreciation can.

Pay attention to great recognition ceremonies.

BECOME A STUDENT OF RECOGNITION

When you watch the Olympics or an award show on TV, take note of how they present their awards. Millions tune in to watch Olympians receive their medals, anticipating and sharing the emotion of the moment. Likewise, our employees long for a little of that emotion in their recognition celebrations.

As you study great recognition moments, and model your award presentations after them, you will soon become a master (who is studied by others).

"Nine tenths of wisdom is APPRECIATION.
Go find somebody's hand and squeeze it . . .
while there's still time!"

— *Dale Denton, naturalist*

GIVE THEM A HAND — YOURS!

Don't wait until it is too late to show your appreciation. Society of Human Resource Management statistics show that 79 percent of people leave their jobs due to lack of recognition.

Don't let your good people get away simply because you didn't take the time to recognize their contributions.

Remember special occasions.

HAPPY BIRTHDAY, STAN!

Enter the birthdays of your employees on a calendar and never let one of the dates pass without a card or other expression — taking the person to lunch, bringing them a cup of coffee in the morning, etc.

Letting your people know you care about them as individuals is a sure-fire way to build a team environment and foster greater collaboration.

When you do something for an employee's family, you become family.

Personalize the work experience.

RECOGNIZE THE NEW MOM OR DAD

It's important to let your employees know you care about them on a personal level — to create a connection past the workplace. When an employee has a baby, it is a wonderful opportunity to send a thoughtful gift — like an illustrated picture book — to the person's home as congratulations.

Make it a recognition moment by including a hand-written note of thanks for the person's accomplishments. Then, in the front of the book, write the baby's name and a brief message, and sign your name.

Take this one step farther by recognizing the new grandpa or grandma.

Acknowledge all work anniversaries.

DON'T LET THIS DAY GO BY WITHOUT THANKS

Enter the work anniversaries of your employees on your calendar, and never let those days go by without a card or other mention. Surveys show people remember the date they were hired at work more easily than they remember their own wedding anniversary date. Do you think your spouse would like it if you didn't remember that date? (Hint: your employees won't either.)

Put a special logo on their business cards.

THE MARK OF SUCCESS

They're good at what they do — and they can prove it.

Motivate employees to meet specific corporate performance goals by reprinting their business cards with a specially designed logo when they do. The key is to set the goal high enough that the logo remains fairly exclusive. Also, resist the urge to use the logo for anything else.

Make it rare, make it valuable — And they'll want to make it their own.

**"Mr. Scorpio says productivity is up 2 percent and
it's all because of my motivational techniques, like donuts —
and the possibility of more donuts to come!"**

— *Homer Simpson, cartoon character and philosopher*

THE PROMISE OF GOOD THINGS TO COME

To our great relief, Homer Simpson is a unique breed of person. But it turns out he's an even more unusual manager.

In our initial visits with corporate leaders across America, we frequently ask how many managers within their corporations actively recognize their workers.

"Maybe 10 to 20 percent," most CEOs reply.

That means if you are recognizing, you've got a strategic advantage over 80 to 90 percent of the managers in your company. Make the most of it. Be different. Be innovative. With recognition. (And, come to think of it, a few strategically placed donuts might not be such a bad idea, either.)

They don't always just go away.

THE DISENCHANTED EMPLOYEE

When an employee is dissatisfied, he has two choices: leave or stay. It's bad when they leave; but it can be worse when they stay.

According to research by The Gallup Organization, only 29 percent of the North American work force is "actively engaged" in their jobs. That means 71 percent of your work force is just doing enough to get by.

Going through their days in a sort of half-sleep, taking the easy way out, avoiding challenges and responsibility, they sap the creative energy and enthusiasm of your entire department.

What's a manager like you to do? You've got two choices.

Put your heads together.

HAVE A BRAINSTORMING MEETING

Have a monthly brainstorming meeting outside of work. Share ideas and thoughts, and recognize at least one person for their innovation. Talk about the ideas and improvements this person has brought to your workplace.

"Don't let the future be held hostage to the past."

— Neal A. Maxwell, religious leader

START ANEW

Songwriter Bob Dylan wrote, "The times, they are a changin'."
And you can, too.

Do what you were hired to do: Lead the way toward your company goal.
Using the right tool for today's business climate — recognition.

Is your office family friendly?

MAKE A WORKING MOM'S DAY

A great reward for an employee with kids is a printed notice allowing her to take a couple of hours off for the next school activity without it counting against vacation time.

Recognize and reward milestone achievement.

A COMPANY CONNECTION

Set department goals for certification, standards, attendance, etc., and present appropriate items with your company logo when employees reach the milestones.

For example, a manager at a factory may present a company jacket when an employee reaches a certain level of technical certification. A manager in an office environment might present a desk item with a company logo to employees who reach a comparable skill level.

People love to know what is going on.

IN THE KNOW

Employees like to hear things straight from the horse's mouth. And in this case, the horse (ahem!) just happens to be your company president.

The next time an issue arises that causes particular concern or curiosity among employees, invite the boss to a department staff meeting to answer employee questions.

Make the most of the moment by taking time to introduce each staff member to the executive by name and briefly praising employees in front of the manager, so he or she can hear.

Be careful what you praise …
because you'll get more of it!

REWARD WHAT IS MOST IMPORTANT

A wards should recognize only results that are important to the organization. You might think this is a case of stating the obvious; but, then, you'd be surprised.

All of us have known a manager who claims to value teamwork but rewards the person with the best individual performance; or a manager who wants her senior sales staff to mentor and train junior employees but rewards salespeople based solely on their personal performance; or a university dean who wants his professors to continually improve their teaching abilities but rewards and recognizes professors only for their research and publications.

No matter what you say, employees will do what you reward.

APRIL

"Achievement seems to be connected with action.
Successful men and women keep moving.
They make mistakes, but they don't quit."

— *Conrad Hilton, founder, Hilton Hotels*

AWARD SUCCESS. LEARN FROM FAILURE.

We wanted to call this page "Accept Failure." It sounds terrible, we know, but it is something that the greatest managers have done.

Let us explain. Successful managers accept that no one is going to get it right 100 percent of the time; we all fail. With this in mind, they have found ways to learn from failures as well as triumphs.

Because they — and the people on their staffs — do not fear failure, it frees them up to try new things, to be creative, to think outside the box — and, ultimately, to succeed.

As managers and leaders, we must ensure that the people with whom we work feel comfortable coming to us with problems and failures. It is how they grow and learn. If your employees know they will be celebrated for success, it will breed excitement. If they know they can come to you with failure — without fear — it will breed trust.

Remember what your people like.

KEEP TRACK OF LIKES AND DISLIKES

They say an elephant never forgets. Well, neither does a good leader. In a notebook or computer file, take note of the types of awards, gifts or other rewards that each person on your team seems to enjoy … and those they don't. That way, you can tailor awards to fit the specific needs of the person you are honoring.

Not only will employees enjoy their rewards more, but it communicates that you are paying attention.

Take recognition to the next level.

PAYING THEIR DUES

Reward a fitness fanatic by paying for his gym dues for a month, or maybe a year. It's a "perpetual" award. Every time the employee works out, they think about who is paying for the membership. And it's the kind of thoughtful recognition that makes it hard to jump ship.

Strike up the band!

MAKE A COMMOTION

At the headquarters of one fast-food giant, those being recognized get a visit from the "recognition band." Band members are employees who grab kazoos, bongos and other noisemakers and make a dramatic trip to the person's cubicle.

That's one company that knows it's okay to make a lot of noise about employee success.

What makes recognition work?

ELEMENTARY, MY DEAR WATSON!

I t's no mystery why some recognition is more effective than others. Just follow these clues:

- Be timely
- Be specific
- Be sincere
- Be prepared

By taking a few minutes to prepare and by using a few helpful techniques, your day-to-day recognition moments (and your formal-recognition events) can do much more than simply thank employees for their contributions; they can enhance working relationships and increase feelings of loyalty and commitment.

"Money is a great motivator, but not a good satisfier."

— *David Klinger, vice president of organizational development,*
Mount Clemens General Hospital

MONEY HAS LITTLE VALUE AS AN AWARD

We all need more money. Just ask any employee what they want and they will almost always say "money." The problem is, it doesn't last. Not in their pockets — and not in their memories.

In a survey by American Express, when 1,010 people were asked what they did with their last cash bonus, almost 30 percent answered that they paid bills. Eighteen percent said they couldn't remember. That's almost half the recipients saying that their last cash bonus had little or no impact, which makes money a lousy award.

Is money important? Of course it is. It's what gets people in the door every day. It's just not what keeps them fully engaged in their work.

On the other hand, recognition done right has a huge emotional impact. You may not remember what you did with your last cash bonus, but we guarantee you remember your last award ceremony.

REMEMBER: Keep cash in your compensation strategy; but keep it out of your recognition program. It makes an awful award.

You can't give what you don't have, soooo ...

GO AHEAD, INDULGE YOURSELF

Today, take the time to refresh your attitude and outlook on work. Treat yourself to that gooey cookie or new page-turner novel for the hard work you have put in over the last week. As you enjoy the reward, see if there isn't someone else in your organization who deserves (or needs) the same treatment.

A new outlook. Get it and then give it away. Great attitudes are meant to be shared.

On this day in history ...

(NOT) A TRIVIAL PURSUIT

To spice up a birthday recognition moment, dig up historical facts that occurred on that date and share them with your team. Or find out what famous people share the same birthday. ("Tori Spelling and Jim Nabors? Cool!")

It may seem a small thing, but it's well worth your small investment of time. Knowing the boss put time and effort into their birthday presentation pays big dividends in employee currency.

And it's kind of fun to remember when bell bottoms were in style and Farrah Fawcett was the all the rage.

Food is the way to an employee's heart.

SPECIAL DELIVERY! SPECIAL DELIVERY!

Deliver candy or healthy snacks to your troops on a certain day every week. Take the delivery time as an opportunity to learn what your people are working on and to recognize their good behavior.

Make the most of formal awards already in place.

CREATING FORMAL MEMORIES

Chances are, your company already has formal service awards. You may even have formal awards for above-and-beyond performance, sales and/or safety. Make the presentation of these awards as meaningful as possible.

Award presentations should be some of the most memorable experiences in your employees' work lives. Done right, they will bond employees to your organization. All it takes is a little preparation, sincerity and specificity.

Check with your HR department to find out when your next employee will receive his or her service award. About a week before, spend a few minutes preparing remarks and asking coworkers to speak. Make this employee's day special, and your investment in time and energy will come back to you tenfold.

In short, don't wing it. This day means too much to the person being honored.

"A soldier will fight long and hard for a bit of colored ribbon."

— *Napoleon Bonaparte, Emperor of the French*

GIVE THEM A REASON

It's a battlefield out there. What are your corporate soldiers fighting for? If you can't answer that question, chances are, neither can they.

Now is a good time to schedule a meeting to go over your company values and mission statement. Make it fun. Make it relate to real life by talking about what activities are most valued in your department, and what types of specific behaviors will garner recognition.

Armed with this knowledge, employees will be better prepared to bring home a victory.

Nothing lasts forever.

NOT EVEN YESTERDAY'S RECOGNITION

Verbal praise or thanks should be given to every employee at least once a week. It doesn't always need to be public, but it never hurts if it's within earshot of other employees. Recognition is not meant to be a secret, it's meant to be shared.

Remember, thank them for specific actions that help achieve your department goals.

It's for a worthy cause (theirs and yours).

DONATE TO THEIR FAVORITE CHARITY

To honor an outstanding employee, make a contribution to her favorite charity. Some managers get this messed up and make a contribution to the company's favorite charity, or worse yet, *their* favorite. But recognition isn't about you. A personal charitable reward should benefit a cause about which the employee feels passionately.

Step up your recognition program.

GET A MOVE ON

Have a walking contest to get everyone healthy. Hand out pedometers when the challenge is introduced. Then reward those who walk the most steps with a bronzed-shoe award.

Recognition can be a matter of opinion.

ASK WHAT THEY THINK

It's tax day in the U.S. You pay, and no one at the IRS ever asks if you think it's okay. Well, here's a little rebellion: ask for opinions on projects you are working on. This shows employees that their ideas are important and valid, and, of course, you'll get some great ideas you wouldn't have thought of on your own.

*"You have to be able to listen well
if you are going to motivate the people who work for you."*

— *Lee Iacocca, American industrialist*

LISTEN UP!

Shhh! Do you hear that? It's the sound of your employees telling you exactly how to motivate them to their highest performance level. Are you listening?

You should be.

Remember the movie *What Women Want?* Mel Gibson's character could hear women's thoughts. When he fought it, it caused him unimaginable grief. When he finally paid attention — it changed his whole world for the better.

And it can do the same for you.

Listen when employees express concerns. Pay attention when they share new ideas. Tune in when they're talking about some great program at another company. It's more than idle talk. It's a road map to success.

"He don't know me vewry well, do he?"

— *Bugs Bunny, cartoon character*

MAKE IT A FAMILY, NOT A TEAM

Try this: think of your employees as a family, not a team. Family is much more definable than team — especially as it relates to roles. Family has a much better feeling of belonging and much stronger as it pertains to tasks and responsibilities. And a family can have a few misfits who can do a great job without feeling like outcasts.

I have found, that if I treat my employees the same as I treat my children and grandchildren, they have a greater sense of belonging and feel more appreciated. I give them "protected, fun, educational, living" benefits, just like I would my kids: memberships in AAA so they don't get stuck on the side of the road at night with a flat tire, Sam's Club and Costco memberships, memberships in the YMCA so they can exercise and be healthy. And, of course, we have parties and outings. We celebrate. And every celebration makes us a better family.

"And here's a bonus thought as you try to move your company to a new level of excellence: Treat your employees BETTER than you treat customers. If you do this, every employee will be in a mood to provide service excellence as a way of life, rather than a chore."

— *submitted by Jeffrey Gitomer*

Foster collaboration by pitching in.

PERFORM A RANDOM ACT OF KINDNESS

Look around your workplace and find a way to help one of your employees or a colleague without their asking. Perhaps you can take an employee's calls or pick up a little of their extra work.

Managers in today's workplace must maximize cooperative efforts. When your people understand they must work together, the results are always better. The best way to build a collaborative environment is to be willing to roll up your sleeves and do a little of their work now and then.

"I resemble that remark!"

— Curly Howard, actor

MAKE SOMEONE GREAT TODAY!

What if employees were like putty in your hands? What if you could simply mold their workplace behaviors and priorities to match your own?

Well, you can. Each time we praise people, they strive to further develop the abilities you have recognized. Praise them for meeting deadlines and they'll be early next time. Did you ever imagine you had such power? Go ahead. Make someone great today!

There's something about wearing jeans to work.

LOOSEN UP (YOUR DRESS STANDARD)

Have a casual Friday to recognize a significant team accomplishment. You can learn a lot about an individual by the clothes he or she chooses to wear to be comfortable. And they'll get to know you better, as well. And . . . you get to say to your boss, "Hey, nice pants."

Have you forgotten someone?

DO A QUICK HEAD COUNT

Spend a few minutes thinking about your team. Think about each member—full or part time, telecommuters, road warriors and those in distant locations. Are there members of your team who you never publicly recognize? Why not?

Don't underestimate the power of laughter.

SHOOTING THE WORKS

On a casual day, organize a department water-gun fight in the parking lot in honor of one of your outstanding employees. Bring the water guns and let people have at it. The only rule is that you must join in.

They'd bend over backwards
to help the company succeed.

GIVE THEM THE GIFT OF FLEXIBILITY

She's always on top of things but at a price. Sometimes she spends her lunch hour at her desk. She often comes in early; and you've caught her here on weekends.

She doesn't make a big deal about it. But maybe it's time you did.

Here's a way to show that you've noticed her extra efforts while giving her greater flexibility and control over her time: a laptop computer. Make it a lasting reminder of your regard by personalizing it with an inscribed plaque.

Let them report directly to your boss.

GIVE THEM VISIBILITY

Have a great employee report directly to the CEO on an important project. This type of face time with the head honcho is one of the best rewards many employees can receive. And it shows you can identify talent and aren't afraid to let them shine.

The Dirty Dozen of Why We Don't

EXCUSE NO. 4

"MY PEOPLE GET THEIR RECOGNITION IN THEIR PAYCHECKS. THAT'S ENOUGH!"

If you believe that, your employees probably gave you this book! And while you're correct that money is why they show up for work each day, it's no indicator of the quality of their work. We need money, but we crave recognition.

Get more than their mere presence. Capture their hearts, souls and minds with recognition.

Send it upwards too.

PRAISE YOUR BOSS

When we do radio call-in shows, one of the most frequently asked questions is, "My boss is terrible at this. How do I get him to start recognizing me?" One great way to start the cycle is by recognizing your boss for the good things he does.

Senior leaders need love too. And a sincere note of thanks or even verbal praise will go a long way. First, your boss will feel better about his role in the organization—knowing he is seen in a positive light by his employees. Second, he will begin to see the role recognition can play in motivating others.

Make sure everyone gets the message.

COMING THROUGH LOUD AND CLEAR

Announce a great accomplishment over the loudspeaker at work, without identifying the employee. Wait a few seconds for the suspense to build. Then get back on and broadcast the employee's name and additional accolades.

We love to hear our names spoken aloud. There is power in a name. Use it

"You didn't say the magic word."

— *Bill Murray, actor, in* Ghostbusters

MIND YOUR Ps AND Qs

As the boss, what you say goes. But it doesn't mean you shouldn't express it politely.

In our travels, we are surprised how often common courtesies have been abandoned in favor of barking orders and giving curt nods.

"Please" and "thank you" are the most basic forms of recognition. They communicate mutual respect and regard, which, in turn, inspires employee loyalty.

Make it a habit to use these two magic words on all occasions with your staff.

Let your employees wear recognition on their sleeves
(and everywhere else).

DRESSED FOR (CONTINUED) SUCCESS

Reward a younger employee with a business outfit of her choice. Send her to the mall and have her bring back the receipts.

Everyone enjoys looking good. It not only helps with attitude but also posture. People who feel good actually hold themselves better and look taller. Go figure.

*"I have yet to find a man,
however exalted his station,
who did not do better work and put forth greater effort
under a spirit of approval
than under a spirit of criticism."*

— *Charles Schwab, chairman of Charles Schwab Corporation*

SCHEDULE A PRAISE SESSION

We never cease to be amazed by the power of praise, and, conversely, by how few managers tap it. Here's a great way to start:

Schedule a one-on-one meeting with an employee to focus on only the positive things that the employee does. Resist the urge to talk about any areas that need improvement. Trust us, it will be difficult. But, then, most truly worthwhile things are.

MAY

For the do-it-yourselfers among us ...

CREATE A HALL OF FAME FILE

We each have a file at the office that isn't opened much but proves invaluable every time we do. We call it the "Hall of Fame File."

It's filled with positive performance appraisals, thank-you cards, awards, personal notes from family and friends — anything that validates us as people and professionals. (Of course, there's always room for more.)

On days when we really need a little emotional pick-me-up or self-esteem booster but none seems to be forthcoming from those around us, we open the file and voila! — instant recognition!

"Can we fix it? Yes we can!"

— *Bob the Builder, cartoon character*

KNOCK YOUR SPOUSE'S SOCKS OFF

There are some times when taking work home (or at least something from it) is a good idea. Tonight is one of those times.

Recognition isn't just for the office. Done frequently and sincerely, it can improve our relationships, even patch up painful rifts. Think about it: appreciation breeds respect. And respect is the foundation of any loving relationship.

Want to knock your spouse's socks off? This evening, when she walks in the door, give her a big hug and kiss (first thing, before anything else) and thank her for something — anything. Just remember, your praise must be sincere.

You won't believe the difference it will make.

*"The smallest change in perspective can transform a life.
What tiny attitude adjustment might turn your world around?"*

—*Oprah Winfrey, celebrity*

READY FOR A CHANGE?

The father of electricity (and insulated kite string), Benjamin Franklin once created a list of thirteen virtues to live by. It included temperance, silence, order, resolution, frugality, industry, sincerity, justice, moderation, cleanliness, tranquility, chastity and humility.

Franklin, who was constantly seeking to improve himself, would choose one of these virtues and work toward improvement in that area before selecting another. In this way, he constantly bettered himself. We'd be wise to follow suit.

In what way could you polish up your recognition skills? Frequency? The presentation? The slightest change in your perspective and abilities could not only transform your experience as a manager but also charge the entire workplace environment.

Set his sights even higher.

WRITE HIS NAME IN THE SKY

At the next company picnic, hire a sky writer to put the name of a star employee in the clouds! Make sure you get a picture of it and frame it for a later presentation

Get points for presentation.

MAKE A GREAT IMPRESSION

Imagine with us. There's starlight and a full moon. Soft music drifts on the breeze from the house. You and your beloved are swinging in the porch swing. Nowhere to go. Nothing to do. The time is right. You get down on one knee and . . . and struggle to . . . pull the wrinkled shopping bag from your pocket. Extracting a small square box from the bag, you hold it up and pop it open. Almost as if on cue, the moonlight falls across it, clearly illuminating . . . a 75-percent-off clearance tag!

So, what do you think her answer will be? (As for us, we know we'll never make that mistake again.)

The point is, presentation counts. So much so, that a survey of more than 33,000 award recipients revealed that the award presentation affects employees' perception of not only the award but the entire recognition program — and even their perception of the company as a whole.

Learn from the pain of so many who have gone before. Don't leave it on their desks. Don't hand it to them still in the shipping wrap. Do spend the time to make it perfect, memorable and inspiring. And remember: proper award presentation means never having to say, "I'm sorry."

"The top 20 percent must be loved, nurtured
and rewarded in the soul and wallet
because they are the ones who make magic happen . . .
and be sure that the high-performance 70 percent
is always energized to improve and move upward."

Jack Welch, former CEO of General Electric

FILL THEIR WALLETS — AND THEIR SOULS

The wallet and the soul, the two keys to motivating people. When you pay people fairly and provide constant recognition, you meet their most basic needs. And that frees them up to give their very best efforts back to you.

In short, money gets them to work. Recognition gets the best out of them at work.

Sounds important!

IT'S NOT JUST A TITLE. IT'S RECOGNITION!

Show an employee you appreciate his efforts by letting him select his own title. Executive Vice Director of Welding Enhancement is a great one we've seen.

Consider ordering business cards incorporating the title for a future award.

Stop the presses!

GET IT IN THE REPORT

As a reward, have an employee's picture included in the annual report. Locate it either in the section discussing outstanding achievement or as a background photo. When it's printed, have it framed and signed with thanks from the CEO. This is a great keepsake and a way to bind a person to the company!

"We applaud each little success one after another —
and the first thing you know they actually become successful.
We praise them to success!"

— *Mary Kay Ash, founder, Mary Kay Cosmetics*

THE POWER OF BELIEVING

Not all top performers are born that way. Some are built — using recognition. There is power in appreciation. The North American work force has hidden reserves of ingenuity, talent and resolve that are just waiting to be tapped. But it takes the right motivator and the right leader, with the right vision.

And it looks like you might just be the right person for the job.

Don't wait for a formal event.

BREAK FOR BAGELS – AND RECOGNITION

Have a department break in honor of one of your outstanding employees. Buy the donuts or bagels and publicly recognize this great person. Take time to explain what values she lives that makes her great.

Recognition never goes out of style.

FOR BETTER OR FOR WORSE

The great thing about carrots is that they're always in season.

When times are good in your company, effective presentations give you a chance to celebrate and reflect. And, unlike monetary rewards that dry up when times are tight, carrots can be used during downturns to bring you closer together and give you hope that better times lie ahead.

(Now, if only the National Hockey League season could last as long.)

Recognition can prep employees for ISO certification.

QUALITY TIME

Reward those who follow your Quality Policies. Rewarding quality is a great way to get everyone aligned for an ISO certification.

*"You can make more friends in two months
by becoming interested in other people than you can in
two years by trying to get other people interested in you."*

— *Dale Carnegie, author and trainer*

BE INTERESTED IN "THEM"

You've got to love the self-centered woman at the bar who is overheard saying, "Yes, well, enough about me . . . what do you think of my dress?"

Often, as managers and leaders, we think the workplace should revolve around us. After all, we are at the top and people should be interested in what we do and what we think. Wrong! As leaders we need to be interested in the people working with us.

What do you really know about your people? Do you know their hobbies and passions? Any pets? Family members?

What you don't know can hurt you, especially when creating recognition moments. Imagine giving a bottle of champagne to an employee who doesn't drink! Sound stupid? It was. We know because Chester was the employee. And it happens all the time to managers who don't know their people.

Recognition is communication. When you take time to get to know your people, it communicates that you care.

Present service awards with more impact.

TALK ABOUT THE FIVE VIRTUES

When presenting a service award, think of the five things that make an employee valuable:

1. Integrity

2. Ability

3. Knowledge

4. Experience

5. Commitment

Lacking any one of these qualities diminishes one's value, sometimes completely. So, find a way to reinforce these "employee virtues" in reference to the person being honored.

Keep your eye on the calendar.

A FORMAL AFFAIR

When it comes to formal recognition, just how often is often enough? Here's the scoop: formal rewards — from company milestone awards to performance and service awards — should be presented at least annually to the majority of your team members. Most sophisticated companies we work with ensure that 40 percent of their work force receives formal awards for outstanding performance at least once a year.

Blending the home and the office.

MAKE IT A FAMILY EVENT

Invite the family of a recognized person to attend a recognition event in his honor. Performance awards, service awards, sales awards and other recognition are wonderful opportunities to bring family members in to work. And remember, a retirement celebration should never be held without the honoree's family in attendance. You can even ask those family members to add a few words of their own.

Goofy awards keep work fun.

ON THE LIGHT SIDE

Create a unique traveling award — we've seen rubber chickens, stuffed animals, planks of wood, and all sorts of odd things — that means something to your organization. For example, the person who has the rubber chicken this week was voted the most flexible the week before. Kind of goofy, we know. But these are the types of things that keep work fun.

*"Have confidence that if you have done a little thing well,
you can do a bigger thing well, too."*

— *David Storey, novelist and playwright*

MOVING IN THE RIGHT DIRECTION

What if football fans reserved their applause for a touchdown or field goal only. No one yelled encouragement. No giant foam No. 1 hands waving in the air. No enormous painted bellies. It would take away a lot of the fun and excitement. And much of the players' motivation.

The same goes for the office. Don't hold back recognition until a project's completion. Celebrate the little landmarks along the way. Recognize small achievements that move you in the right direction. The momentum you create will help carry you toward your ultimate goal.

And if you come in with your stomach painted blue ... well, good for you.

Remember the times you were recognized?

SHARE THE MOMENT

Show your employees that company values aren't just for the line workers; they impact management's work, too.

To do this, schedule time during staff meeting to talk about the times you have been recognized for living the corporate values. Explain how those same values impact your choices today.

The Dirty Dozen of Why We Don't

EXCUSE NO. 5

"BUT THEY WILL EXPECT MORE PRAISE!"

Let me see if I've got this straight. They perform. You give praise. They perform again. You give praise again. Hoping to get more praise, they perform again. And that's a bad thing?

Here's the real problem: generic, perfunctory praise that comes across as insincere. Get involved, be specific and lay it on . . . meaningful praise, that is.

There's no better strategy.

GET THEM INVOLVED

The next time you meet for a high-level strategy session, ask to invite an outstanding employee to participate. Sometimes the best recognition is involvement in the meetings that impact the employee's work. It shows you respect their ideas and talents and gives them personal ownership in the company's overall direction.

When your opinion matters, you matter, and the more engaged you'll be.

"Recognition is like a small drop of oil in
the machinery of business...
it just makes things run a little smoother."

— *Obert C. Tanner, founder, recognition industry*

RUNNING MORE SMOOTHLY

Obert Tanner realized this in 1940, when he recognized the need for corporations to reward their people with service awards. For Obert, recognition revolved around the Golden Rule — do unto others as you would have them do unto you. And it served him well.

Ask yourself, don't you feel better about your work life when you are receiving praise and recognition on a regular basis? Don't you think your employees want that drop of oil in their lives too?

Recognition can help you spot their strengths.

GET AN ACCURATE APPRAISAL

Recognition can help you better evaluate team members' strengths and weaknesses. Think about what you would recognize about each employee and what you wouldn't. If you want, identify areas for improvement from the list you develop.

"According to the American Psychological Association, 'equitable rewards and recognition' are one of the top 12 most essential characteristics for a healthy company culture."

— Workforce Magazine

JUST DO IT!

Everyone knows that the secret of good physical health is a balanced diet, regular exercise and proper nutrition. Unfortunately, it isn't the knowing that makes it happen. The difference lies in the doing.

What are you doing about recognition? Chances are, if you're reading this book, you know the importance of recognition. And that's a start. However, your department culture will become healthier only when you implement the principles from this book.

To quote a well-known sportswear manufacturer, you don't even have to do it well, at first, as long as you "just do it!"

Let them eat cake!

USE YOUR CUSTOMER'S PRODUCTS

Does one of your clients or customers produce a product you could use as an award? If so, order some for your next recognition event. We used Sara Lee cakes as a team thank-you and people loved it!

The benefits of this approach are twofold: your employees get the recognition they deserve, as well as a subtle reminder of the importance of your valued clients.

(FYI: If your client is BMW, you are going to be one popular person!)

You get out what you put in.

FEED BACK THE POSITIVES

You know, you can never get too much of a good thing. Especially if it's positive feedback.

Document the good things you hear from customers or other employees about a member of your staff. Share that information with the employee during her annual review.

Third-party customer praise is powerful stuff, helping you reinforce the values of service, relationship-building and loyalty.

You wouldn't believe how much
that little note means.

MORE PRECIOUS THAN GOLD

It wasn't worth more than a couple cents, if that. We could have gone down to the store and bought a whole pack any day of the week and covered ourselves with them. But somehow none of that mattered.

All we knew is that we wanted that gold star from our teacher. And we wanted it bad.

That's the same way most of us feel about a simple hand-written note of appreciation from our boss. As we visit client locations, we've seen personal cards from supervisors posted on cubicles and office walls throughout North America. Why? Because recognition is rare and valuable. And we crave it.

Today, send a note of thanks to one of your employees.

Choose an award that fits the employee.

WHEN IN DOUBT, ASK

We once met with a company that was considering taking system-wide a seemingly successful sales-performance program they had launched in one division. The winner of the sales contest had been presented with a wonderful trip to an exotic locale. In the course of our work with the firm, we discovered that the man had never taken the trip. Of course, we asked why.

"I'm terrified of flying," he replied.

A lot of the time, you can avoid problems like this through frequent department walk-throughs and careful observation and listening. But when in doubt about the appropriateness of an award, ask. Ask the employee's spouse. Ask his coworkers. Ask the employee himself.

"I am certain that after the dust of centuries
has passed over our cities, we, too, will be remembered
not for victories or defeats in battle or in politics,
but for our contribution to the human spirit."

— *John F. Kennedy, former president of the United States*

HOW WILL YOU BE REMEMBERED?

It's been said that we should plan our lives in reverse. What we mean is, we should think about what we would want people to say at our funerals and then work on getting there.

With that perspective, you might want to change a few things about how you treat the people around you. Take care to look for the good in people and recognize and reward it. Does that mean you never give anyone bad news or a poor evaluation? Of course not. It means you look for the best first, and when you have to make corrections you do it with dignity and caring. In the long run, it will be remembered in a positive way, no matter the outcome.

Begin today to make time for the important conversations — those that lift, reward and motivate the people around you.

Say it with flowers (a roomful).

100 ROSES!

Want to say congratulations in a spectacular way? Send 100 roses home or to the office to celebrate a promotion or exceptional job. It may sound corny, but we've done it and the reaction is SPECTACULAR! It looks great, feels great and smells great — the trifecta of recognition

There are several online flower brokers that can provide this at affordable prices to create a once-in-a-lifetime experience.

Relaxing with a bucket of balls.

RAGE ON THE RANGE

Nothing releases stress like hitting a bucket of balls on the driving range. Let your employees take out their rage on the range as a reward.

Of course, you don't want to do it too often or they'll make their home on the range. Okay, okay. We know. That was awful. Turn the page . . . quickly.

JUNE

Make an appointment with yourself.

SQUEEZE IT INTO YOUR SCHEDULE

On Monday, write in your day planner that you will publicly recognize someone on your team this week. You can move it to another day, but it has to be completed by Friday.

*"In the most innovative companies,
there is a significantly higher volume of thank-yous
than in companies of low innovation."*

— *Rosabeth Moss Kanter, Harvard Business School professor*

RECOGNITION BREEDS INNOVATION

We've found the missing link ... to innovation! (And, since you're reading this book, so have you.)

No surprise here — it's recognition. And it just makes sense, really. People are like wells. When they give and give and give their best ideas, and get little or nothing in return, they run dry. Recognition refreshes an employee's spirit of innovation and fills them with the desire to give more!

Don't want to end up a dinosaur in your industry? The key is recognition.

Feed their inner child.

SET A PLAY DATE

Reward a team by offering a workday that includes the best memories of childhood: Pez, Slinky races down the stairs, Silly Putty sculpture contests, spontaneous games of Pic-Up Stix, Twister, Clue or Life. (And don't forget snack time.)

Take your cue from Maslow's Hierarchy of Needs

ON-THE-LEVEL RECOGNITION

You might have studied Maslow's Hierarchy of Needs in college. (Remember Pysch 101?) Well, it's not all academic. Maslow's research can help you determine how to best motivate your employees.

Here's a quick refresher course: In 1954, psychologist Abraham Maslow proposed that people are motivated by a set of internal needs. He arranged these needs into a hierarchy, beginning with the most basic needs and ending with the most sophisticated.

Now, here's the key: when one level of needs is satisfied, it no longer serves as an effective motivator, and the individual is motivated by the next level of needs in the hierarchy.

Ask yourself: Which level of needs are my employees seeking? Assuming your company's pay and benefits are competitive and the workplace is safe, they are seeking to fill their esteem needs.

And that begs the question: What recognition have you provided them lately?

An employee's first day sets the tone.

MAKE IT A BANNER DAY

Surprise a new employee with a welcome banner on the door or over her desk. Make sure you are there to greet her as she arrives and to introduce her to coworkers.

Nine out of ten employees can tell you the date of their first day on the job. What do you want them to remember? A cold and aloof boss, or someone who is really happy to see them?

The Dirty Dozen of Why We Don't

EXCUSE NO. 6

"I DON'T WANT TO GET TOO FRIENDLY WITH MY PEOPLE."

Give me a break! With all the extra hours we put in today, we spend more time at work with our coworkers than at home. You'd better get familiar with your people! The great thing is that recognition helps you do that in a very positive way. Don't worry about familiarity; it's a good thing!

Make the weekly meeting do double duty.

RUNNING THE SHOW

Reward leadership with leadership responsibility: let your high achiever run the weekly meeting. Give the reward of a voice in the meeting and a chance to set the agenda.

JUNE

A CARROT | | A DAY

The best resource for recognition ideas
might be right next door.

ASK AROUND

Ask your neighbors and friends to tell you about their favorite recognition moments — even if they occurred years ago in school. Understanding how people feel when they are recognized can only help make you a better leader.

Help make it her own.

RECOGNITION WITH PERSONALITY

If you have a great new employee or you have an employee who has just been promoted and is in a new office, reward her with a shopping spree to a local mall to customize her space. We'd all like to show our personality in our office space, it's just that most of us can't afford to. But hey, if the boss is paying.

The next-best thing to a stadium.

PUT THEIR NAME ON THE DOOR

How would it feel to have a building named after you? Give your outstanding employee a peek into the world of the rich and famous by naming the boardroom after them for a specified period of time. (It's especially nice if it's the one where company big-wigs regularly meet.)

Put a gold plaque on the door. And don't forget to snap a photo of the employee standing next to their namesake.

"Try not. Do, or do not. There is no try."

— *Yoda,* Star Wars *character*

DO IT!

There are a million reasons why you really should put off recognition until tomorrow. You have so much to do. You haven't had time to fully prepare. Believe us, we've been there. We know what you're talking about.

Now, put all that aside — simply decide to ignore all the excuses — and go do it!

Start writing thank-you cards today. Call a short staff meeting and make a recognition presentation — today. Now is the time to begin. There is no better opportunity.

Make today a "DO" day.

Cultivate the seeds of commitment and loyalty.

AN AWARD TO GROW ON

Plant a tree in an outstanding employee's name. To make a real statement, go a little farther. Start a Grove of Champions by planting the tree on the company lawn, with a small (but permanent) name marker. Then add to it. Cool idea, huh? (Get it? Shade? Trees? Cool? Oh, never mind.)

Turnaround is fair play.

RIGHT BACK AT YA

The next time you are recognized, be sure to thank the person who recognized you. Send a hand-written note of thanks expressing why his acknowledgment of your achievement meant so much to you.

Get the picture?

SURPRISE! YOU'RE ON CANDID CAMERA

Keep a small disposable camera in your drawer for spontaneous photos of great moments at work. Catch people working hard and having fun. Use these to create a yearbook of memories for your staff. Present this to your team at year's end.

"All appears to change when we change."

— Henri Amiel, writer

KEEP ON SMILING

Spend today thinking and saying nothing but positive things — at the workplace, at home, even on the commute (gulp). Staying positive during a normal, stressful, challenging day will not be easy, but this exercise will help you be a positive influence on your team in good times and bad.

Let them leave early.

BEAT THE RUSH

For your people who make long, hideous commutes each day, give them the reward of time: let them leave fifteen to thirty minutes early today to get ahead of the game a little.

Give employees an extra day off on their birthdays.

SOMETHING TO CELEBRATE

Work with HR to give employees their birthdays off without it counting against vacation days. It may take a little work, but it is a nice perk. If your birthday falls on a weekend, you get a floating holiday birthday!

Younger workers value inclusion.

X, Y AND M (FOR MOTIVATION)

For the most part, Generation-X and -Y workers are looking for daily proof that their work matters. That means recognition — frequent, meaningful recognition.

HR experts note that despite the media dubbing them slackers, Gen-X and Y employees are typically self reliant and entrepreneurial in spirit. And while it's tough to keep this group motivated, it's not impossible.

First and foremost, Gen-X employees want to be involved in decision making. Forget the days of giving orders or leading the troops by example. To gain the heart and soul of your younger workers, you must learn to lead by interaction and inclusion.

*This approach to recognition gives something
to the community — and you!*

A LOAN WITH PAY BACK

To reward the philanthropic employee, give her a paid sabbatical to help a charitable organization in your community. Many organizations willingly take these loaned executives, and your employee will bring back new skills and a renewed energy to work hard for you.

This hospital makes it easy to say "thanks."

FOR YOUR CONVENIENCE

Nursing can be a thankless job. That's why one hospital makes it easy for patients to express their gratitude.

Along with standard hospital-issue supplies, a hospital we recently visited provides thank-you notes and a pen to each patient. With the tools readily at hand, many patients spend part of their stay expressing gratitude to those who served them.

The notes are placed on a bulletin board for all hospital staff to see.

This health-care company has learned that people work for more than a paycheck. They want to know they have made a difference.

You can't pay people enough to do some jobs.

IT'S ALL ABOUT RECOGNITION

It's not money that drives people away. One recent study showed the average salary differential for job hoppers was a little more than five percent. People don't leave their jobs for money.

Companies with low turnover typically have good managers, and those managers provide employees with challenges, opportunities, and confirmation that they make a difference, supported by recognition and awards.

Provide those, and turnover will fall faster than a pair of cheap socks.

Don't let a moment of praise slip away.
Give employees something ...

TO HAVE AND TO HOLD

When you praise or recognize an employee, type up what you said during the recognition moment and place a copy in the employee's personnel file. When review time comes up, talk about the recognition again.

For an employee that's an exceptionally rare find ...

AN AWARD THAT'S RIGHT ON THE MONEY

Go to a coin collector's shop and find some unusual money — an old penny or some bills from their ancestral homeland. It's a unique, colorful (and not that expensive) gift. Make it an award for a cost-saving idea or give it to someone who has found an unusual way to generate profit or save money.

Make a list and check it twice.

LONG TIME, NO RECOGNITION

When you get into the habit of giving recognition frequently, it's easy to lose track of whom you have recognized and, more importantly, whom you haven't.

It's like the man we heard of who loved to give away books with a personal inscription written inside. One day, after receiving a book from this generous fellow, the recipient said, "I thoroughly appreciate this book. It is the third copy you have given me."

Take a recognition inventory of the people you work with. When was the last time you gave any of them some positive feedback? Like Santa, make a list and check it twice to ensure your praise is equitable.

Share the credit.

RECOGNITION. PASS IT ON.

When you give a presentation to senior management or a speech to a group, be sure to acknowledge everyone on your team who worked on the topic you are addressing. This type of recognition shows management you are a team builder who is willing to share credit. Inevitably, word will leak back to your people that you support them and are looking to build their careers too.

"No act of kindness, no matter how small, is ever wasted."

— Aesop's Fables

THINK IT DIDN'T DO ANY GOOD? THINK AGAIN

If you're anything like the rest of us, not all your attempts at recognition have gone well. Join the club.

We don't know one leader who regularly practices recognition who hasn't experienced a setback or two. At those moments, you may wonder, "Did I mess it up too badly?" or "Was that all just a waste of time?"

The answer is no. And no.

A sincere, heartfelt attempt at recognition is never wasted. If nothing else, you — the presenter — walk away better prepared for the next recognition moment (which, by the way, promises to be so incredible, it will take your breath away).

Never give up.

It's all in the way you look at things.

AN ATTITUDE OF GRATITUDE

Mental note to self: need a change in perspective; make appointment with optometrist.

Wouldn't it be great if it were that easy to alter your general outlook on things? It's not; but it's not impossible, either.

To cultivate a habit of seeing the good in people, we suggest starting a "gratitude journal." Here's how it works: each day, write down all the things you are grateful for (or, in the interest of time, at least one thing you appreciate). It's that simple. There's no need to even buy a journal if you'd rather not (although it might serve as a good motivator or reminder). A file on your computer named "gratitude journal" works just as well.

Actively seeking (and later reviewing) the good things at work and in your personal life will soon become a habit that will benefit you for a lifetime.

"Other things being equal,
the more immediate the reinforcement, the more powerful
it is in terms of strengthening behavior."

— *Paul L. Brown,* Managing Behavior on the Job

MAKE A BIG SPLASH (QUICK!)

In a scene in the Walt Disney film *Peter Pan,* Wendy is forced to walk the plank. As she resolutely leaps from the plank, the pirates listen expectantly for a splash — that never comes.

"No splash!" they cry in shock and panic. "There wasn't any splash!" (Of course, unbeknownst to them, Wendy had been scooped up by Peter Pan and carried to safety.)

The moral: If you're planning to offer recognition, make sure it closely follows the behavior you're recognizing. Your employees are waiting for the splash — your reaction and appreciation. Don't disappoint.

*Can employees outline your
company vision in their sleep?*

THE 2 A.M. TEST

How do you think your employees would fare if given the 2 a.m. test? Haven't heard of it? James Di Loreto at the Catalyst Group describes it this way:

"If you have communicated your mission and values properly, any employee should be able to recite it to you without hesitation, even if awakened at 2 a.m. to do it." Undoubtedly, employee recognition moments provide a prime opportunity to link company mission and values with behavior. Here's how you do it:

1. Reward employees for activities and behaviors that support company values; and

2. Vocalize the link between their behaviors and those values while presenting the award. Here's an example: "Kathy, I want to thank you for finding a way to get that replacement order out by Friday, as promised. It was a great example of 'providing the highest level of customer service,' one of our three company values."

If these steps are second nature, rest assured your employees would pass the 2 a.m. test with flying colors. If not, consider this your wake-up call.

"You have a problem and you will fix it, or I will replace you.
Hell will freeze over before this CEO
implements another employee benefit in this culture ...
You have two weeks. Tick, tock."

— *Neal Patterson, CEO, Cerner*

DON'T EVER TRY THIS AT THE OFFICE

We couldn't resist including this real-life quote, which illustrates how many executives really feel about recognition and awards.

The rest of the story demonstrates why it's killing them: Offended Cerner employees posted Patterson's message on the Web, triggering a 20 percent drop in company stock prices.

(In Patterson's defense, he later apologized to his entire staff.)

JULY

The Dirty Dozen of Why We Don't

EXCUSE NO. 7

"I SHOULDN'T HAVE TO REWARD PEOPLE FOR JUST DOING THEIR JOBS!"

How well people do their jobs depends on your ability as a leader to communicate your expectations. And, it turns out, there's no better way to accomplish that than through recognition.

Contrary to popular belief, no news is not good news at the office. People need to know when they are on the right track. Let them know through recognition.

Like what someone is doing? Reward him publicly. You'll be amazed at how many people start doing the same thing.

So, in short, you aren't just rewarding people for doing their jobs. You are rewarding them for doing their jobs well.

Remember the folks who keep things running smoothly.

THE STEADY EDDY

When it comes to recognition, too many managers get star struck. With their eyes filled with star performers, they overlook the people in the middle, the folks we like to call the Steady Eddys. (Our carrots trainer, Scott Christopher, calls them the Performin' Normans, but he's a little strange).

Anyway, these are the employees who show up every day and do good, solid work. They may not be your top performers, but they are the backbone of your business; and they need encouragement, too.

Who are the Steady Eddys on your staff? Find a way to express your appreciation today.

When employees make big improvements . . .

IMPROVE RELATIONSHIPS WITH THIS GIFT

Now and then, a personalized gift certificate can be thoughtful. For example, a great reward for a new homeowner is a gift certificate to a home-improvement store.

But remember, a gift certificate needs to be applicable and appropriate.

*"You can't know employees as individuals
until you're willing to put in the time to talk to them.
And you have to talk to them
to know what motivates them."*

— *Arthur Pell, author,*
The Complete Idiot's Guide to Managing People

YOU REALLY SHOULD GET OUT MORE!

Stop everything! That's what Dr. Paul Pearsall, author of *Toxic Success* suggests you do first thing every morning.

"Don't check your e-mail or voice mail or go into a meeting. Take one full minute just to sit at your desk and take deep breaths.

"The second step is to connect with the people you will be working with that day. Not to discuss problems or get the agenda rolling, but just to say good morning and chat a minute before you begin work. Having a manager who pays attention to them initially stuns people. They're so used to the rapid pace of the typical office that they're taken aback. But we promise you that the minute you spend chatting with them will pay big dividends later in the day."

After a high-stress assignment, give time to decompress.

SIT BACK AND RELAX

Give an employee a day at a spa as a reward. This type of pampering will be well appreciated and a nice break from the hectic work environment.

She's given you a reason to celebrate, give her ...

A DAY OFF FOR NO REASON AT ALL

When an employee does something worthy of celebration, give her a day off — with absolutely no restrictions. You might want to make up an "I feel too good to come to work today" pass and let your employee use it whenever she chooses.

Think of it as a school hall pass for us grown-ups.

"People work for the money,
but go the extra mile for recognition, praise and rewards."

— *Stuart Levine, CEO, Dale Carnegie and Associates*

REWARDS THAT REALLY GO THE DISTANCE

Want to get the most mileage out of employee efforts? (Bet you can guess what we're going to say.) Organize an employee recognition program.

Research by consulting firm DDI shows that "high-involvement programs," including employee recognition, produce 70 percent better products, services and customer service than when they are lacking. And that's not all. Programs that get employees involved also yield a 65 percent gain in productivity.

Do the math. It adds up to your success.

Tell them you want the good news first.

SHARE YOUR SUCCESSES

Start a staff meeting by asking employees to share something good that happened to them in the last week, either personally or professionally. It's a great way to set a positive tone for your meeting — and it helps build teamwork and a sense of belonging. Of course, don't forget to verbally praise the great work.

When they're hungry for recognition ...

DISH IT UP!

Give a great employee a certificate for dinner for two to his favorite restaurant. The great thing about this type of reward is that it extends recognition to the people who really matter most to him. And you get to pick up the check without even being there.

Recognition that pulls your
work force together, not apart.

GET THE UNION BEHIND YOU

If you manage a unionized work force, you know that favoritism is frowned upon in most labor settings. Thus, here are a few guidelines for improving the manager–union employee relationship and delivering recognition to unionized teams:

- Communicate early. Discuss with your team what rewards you plan to offer and how this is an addition to, not an infringement of, their compensation package.

- Give employees a voice. Let employee teams have a role in choosing rewards (not cash) and reward recipients.

- Reward groups of employees. Instead of rewarding just the best individual, and instead of trying to reward your entire work force, provide an appropriate reward to a three- or four-person team that completes a special project, achieves an accident-free record, develops a new process or in some other way advances the organization's goals.

Give them their pick.

THINKING INSIDE THE BOX

Keep a recognition box in your office. When someone does something great, let her reach into the box and select a surprise — anything from a long lunch break to movie tickets.

NOTE: If someone pulls out a slip of paper that says "free car," there might be some ballot stuffing going on.

Speaking of recognition …

GET AN OUTSIDE POINT OF VIEW

Treat your people to a guest speaker. Bring in someone you known who can share a great idea or a motivational story. It is fun to take some time to hear what others have done to overcome great odds. It is a wonderful team-building experience.

Be careful what you reward, because ...

IT WILL BE REPEATED

Remember, rewards are effective only when they honor the right people for the right behaviors. Allow this type of recognition to become a popularity contest and all strategic benefits evaporate.

Here's an example of a reward nearly gone wrong. The truly frightening part is, it really happened. (But we'll change the names to protect the guilty.)

A vice president we know sat down with his CEO and a list of his customer service managers. The VP had ranked them from one to six. When asked what the ranking involved, he said, "Well, Susan's number one. She gets the new business packets out in the fastest time. They are always very neat."

"Who gets their packages out in the most creative, innovative manner, helping us win the most accounts?" the CEO asked.

He said, "Well, that would be Roger."

Guess where Roger was on the ranking. Near the bottom. His stuff wasn't so neat and on-time, but he closed like a demon.

If the CEO had approved the bonuses as-is, would they have rewarded the right thing? Of course not. What message would they have sent to Roger and his team? Work faster. Be neat. We don't care about winning accounts. Ouch.

The moral? Be careful what you reward because it will be repeated.

How do you spell top performer?

A-B-C-D

Create an A-B-C-D award to be given to a person in your office who goes Above and Beyond the Call of Duty. Since we learned our ABCs in school, the reward could be a basket of fresh apples or even a glass apple.

> *"This brain doesn't contain all the answers,*
> *but I'll know a good one when I hear it.*
> *And I'll recognize that person for it."*

— *Kent Murdock, CEO, O. C. Tanner Company*

HEY, BOSS! DID YOU HEAR THAT?

It's not a leader's job to have all the answers. But it is her job not to let the good ones get away.

Some managers wonder aloud to us why their employees never seem to generate new and innovative ideas, why their companies just seem to stagnate in mediocrity. The answer is this: because employee ideas are not appreciated.

Start a suggestion box. Dedicate part of weekly staff meetings to idea generation. And, of course, publicly recognize people for their ideas.

Recognizing innovative ideas — not just achievements — fosters creativity within the workplace. After all, every employee wants to feel that he or she is making significant contributions in their workplaces. It's up to you to make sure they do.

cc the world!

GET THE WORD OUT

Ever had someone humiliate you by sending a copy of an embarrassing e-mail (cc) to everyone you know? We all have. Turn the tables and cc the world on someone who has done a great job. And we do mean the world! From the CEO to the night guard, let everyone know that something good is happening!

Make an example of her.

LET HER BE A MENTOR

In the children's storybook *Mike Mulligan and His Steam Shovel*, Mike is challenged to dig the basement of the new Popperville town hall in just one day — an unheard-of feat.

As he is beginning, a little boy comes along. "Do you think you will finish by sundown?" he said to Mike Mulligan.

"Sure," said Mike, "if you stay and watch us We always work faster and better when someone is watching us."

Don't we all. Ever noticed how your performance is heightened whenever someone is watching? (How about when a police car is behind you on a city street?)

To reward a great employee, ask her to be a mentor to a new hire. With someone watching and learning from her, she will perform at a higher level and it can help to develop her into a future leader.

*"No person was ever honored for what he received.
Honor has been the reward for what he gave."*

— *Calvin Coolidge, former president of the United States*

IT'S SIMPLE: GIVE.

We sometimes worry that if we praise people too much it will lose its meaning. Please allow us to ease your mind: that will never happen.

Most of us never get enough praise and positive reinforcement. If you really must worry about something, you would do better to worry about whether you are providing enough recognition.

In the most comprehensive study done on workplace environment, The Gallup Organization determined that top performers need positive reinforcement at least once a week. We believe that should be a bare minimum.

REMEMBER: The more you practice constant and frequent recognition, the more it will become second nature. Frequency builds trust, teamwork and relationships that are positive and productive.

When it comes to company values, less is more.

KEEP IT SIMPLE, SUPERVISOR! (K.I.S.S.)

Some companies' corporate values remind us of a kid's Christmas list: way, way too long! We've visited companies that proclaim to have twelve, or even more, key values. Our question to them is "How are employees expected to remember what's important?"

The secret is to keep it simple. Choose three or four values, at most.

Think about it this way: Moses introduced only ten values, and most people have trouble keeping them in mind.

Human nature. Don't fight it. Use it.

WHAT'S IT LIKE TO WANT? MOTIVATING!

It's natural for human beings to want what we don't have. That's why recognition programs work so well: they give employees something to want.

We can picture ourselves wearing a beautiful piece of jewelry or an eye-catching ring. We can imagine just where that stunning Howard Miller mantel clock will go in our home. We understand how handy a Swiss Army knife would be on the next camping trip. Of course, we'd love to have that compact Sony camcorder for when the new baby arrives. And we can visualize ourselves burning up the back nine with those new Callaway golf clubs.

Because we can picture the award and can imagine ourselves enjoying it, we are more likely to work harder to achieve it. It's human nature. (Why not use it to your advantage?)

Capture the moment.

TAKE A SNAPSHOT

Take pictures of a recognition ceremony and give them to the honoree. This is one way to involve family if they are unable to be there.

Photos create a great memory for the employee as well as serving as a constant motivator. And if you put the photos in a nice album or cover, they will be treasured for years to come.

Take an employee to your next client meeting.

PUT A FACE ON YOUR COMPANY — HERS!

When meeting with a client, invite an employee who has worked on the account to join the tour and help answer questions about your company and services. Invite her to join you and the customer for lunch.

This approach to recognition has several advantages: (1) It gives the client a human face, (2) your customer will appreciate getting to know the people behind the scenes, and (3) your employee may feel a renewed commitment to the client.

One important note: make sure the person has a meaningful role in the meeting. The reward is in the confidence that you show in her.

Food for thought.

SOMETHING TO CHEW ON

Think about your first job out of college or high school. How would that first job have been different if the company had properly acknowledged your contributions and created a culture of recognition and encouragement from day one?

Resolve to make that difference for the next employee you hire.

Everything's easier when you have ...

THE RIGHT TOOLS

Celebrate an employee's promotion by giving her something she can use in her new job. It allows you to congratulate her achievement while spurring her toward the next one.

A thank-you for a thank-you.

A REPEAT PERFORMANCE

Recognize employees after you have seen them giving recognition to someone else. The more people who are actively recognizing others, the greater the dividends to your company — and the less stress on you.

> *"When people work in a place that cares about them,*
> *they contribute a lot more than duty."*

— *Dennis Hayes, Hayes Microcomputer Products*

GET MORE OUT OF THEM

We often tell managers that their employees are cold-blooded. Not in a' negative sense, of course. What we mean is that employee energy level and productivity — even attitude — change to match the environment.

A colleague of ours illustrates the point perfectly. The other day, he mentioned two former supervisors. One, named Rama, was skilled at recognition. The other, well . . . wasn't.

"Did I ever work sixty-hour weeks for her [on salary]?" he shook his head. "But I did for Rama."

You see, without external motivators, employees tend to slow down, and their performance can get a little sluggish. In contrast, when recognition is present, they're on top of their game.

So, now, what's the climate like in your department?

This award takes the cup.

SHARE AND SHARE ALIKE

Our favorite sports trophy is Lord Stanley's Cup, the ultimate award for professional hockey. Why? Because when your team wins it, each member gets the cup for a week. Do the same with your team awards and let each team member have the trophy for a week or two to take home to their family, their mom and dad, or even the guys at the bar.

Time is of the essence.

TICK. TOCK. TICK. TOCK.

To be effective, recognition should be timely. That means if you need to get approvals before giving a recognition award, get those in the fastest manner possible. Presentations must be made within a few days or weeks of the accomplishment. Wait longer than that and you've missed your window of opportunity.

Think this might not be a big deal? Ever missed your wedding anniversary by five minutes? Ever missed a loved one's birthday? Then you know what we mean. Being timely is vital.

Frame him.

WHEN THE WRITING'S ON THE WALL

If one of your employees or coworkers is quoted in a business publication, frame the article and present it to him as a memento. It lets the person know it's great when we get our company's name out to the public in a credible manner.

Pay them to party.

HOW WOULD IT BE?

One of our favorite recognition events, by far, is our company's annual picnic at a local amusement/water park. Our company pays the full park admission price for each member of the employee's family and provides a free dinner. But it goes a step farther. We give everyone a half day off to enjoy the event with their family. It's just one of the many ways the company says "thank you."

If your company picnic isn't well attended, consider having it on company time. Somehow the food is sweeter and the conversation is a little more lively when you are getting paid to party! And that feeling of good will can't help but follow employees back to the office.

Rewards should stand for something.

CHARMED, I'M SURE

When you look at your engagement ring or wedding band, what do you see? A ring? Or the love of your life?

We live in a society of symbols. When you give an award, try to attach some symbolism to it. It will make a huge difference in the value of the award years from now. For example, we know of a company that gives a charm every year at the annual sales retreat. Employees and spouses wear the charm with great pride to show how many trips they have been on and to remind them of the great memories associated with each trip. The charms have power.

Symbolism — it's the difference between another "thing" and a lasting memory.

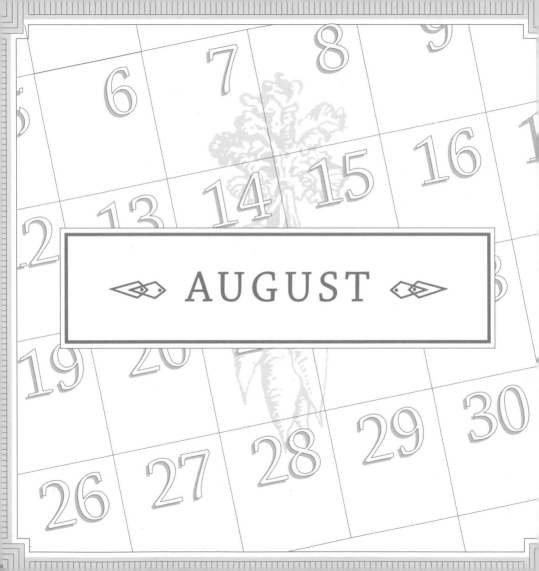

AUGUST

The Dirty Dozen of Why We Don't

EXCUSE NO. 8

"BUT IT MAKES ME FEEL UNCOMFORTABLE."

At first, it probably will. But so do a lot of things of value, like your first exercise session or your first presentation to senior management. So don't worry. Like anything else, the more you do it, the better you'll get. Don't let nerves get in the way of your potential.

Be part of the solution.

HELP!

Sometimes the best way to recognize an employee for achievement is by recognizing that he might need help resolving a personal issue. You can help — while maintaining a healthy on-the-job relationship — by simply providing the resources he needs.

At one business, this involved paying a tax preparer to help employees file their taxes. Another firm with a high percentage of Spanish-speaking workers offered on-site English as a Second Language classes. Another sponsored a weight-loss group. You get the idea.

When employees' personal lives are in order, they are better able to concentrate on the task at hand — helping the company succeed. Caring about someone in a very personal way is the ultimate thank-you.

*"There are only two ways of spreading light —
to be the candle or the mirror that reflects it."*

— *Edith Wharton, novelist*

LIGHT IT UP!

Use your recognition programs to spread the light of accomplishment in your organization. As you do, you will see more satisfaction and dedication reflected in your coworkers' eyes.

Get ready to see some serious results.

WHEN A REWARD WORKS

At one restaurant chain, leaders were losing employees at an alarming rate. Turnover in food service is typically 200 percent or higher a year. And, frankly, company leaders were having a tough time getting their front-line workers — typically sixteen- to twenty-one-year-olds — motivated and excited about the company's goals.

The carrot they picked was relatively simple. When employees were caught doing something right, they were handed a gold coin. (Actually, it was a yellow plastic coin, but they got the idea.) When employees collected enough of these golden treasures, they turned them in for hip merchandise.

The result? Restaurants had to re-lacquer the floors because workers were cleaning them so often. Many of these young people admitted, "Sure, I could get twenty-five cents more an hour over at McDonald's, but I want to get that necklace."

Another not-so-obvious result: through the reward program, workers were starting to understand (and implement) what was important to the company — cleanliness, hospitality and accuracy.

REMEMBER: To be effective, awards must be valued by employees — and given only for the behaviors valued by your company.

Try living dangerously.

THE PAYOFFS OF WORKING THE "PEOPLE SIDE"

Talk about getting no respect. For more than a decade, the "people side" of business has been the Rodney Dangerfield of the corporate boardroom. Ignored. Ridiculed. All but abandoned in favor of leadership by spreadsheet.

But that was then. This is now. Today, more and more managers are recognizing the importance of nurturing their people — and producing hard-to-overlook economic dividends along the way.

In a study of 3,000 companies, researchers at the University of Pennsylvania found that spending 10 percent of revenue on capital improvements raises productivity by 3.9 percent, but a similar investment in developing human capital increases productivity by 8.5 percent — more than twice as much.

When it comes to boosting the bottom line, it looks like the "touchy-feely" side of business might just be the Midas Touch.

Cook up some real results.

YOUR SECRET RECIPE

The next time you set an unusually challenging group goal, up the ante a little. Announce that you will personally cook them breakfast — or barbeque them lunch, whatever is your specialty — when the goal is attained.

The key here is that you actually do the cooking. Don't hand it off to someone else — not even upper management. It seems a small thing, but employees will go to great lengths to see their supervisor slaving away . . . for them. (Now, employees could help with the dishes.)

"No one is useless in this world
who lightens the burden for anyone else."

— *Charles Dickens, author*

BE A TEAM PLAYER

Too many supervisors see themselves as a part of the team — but not really. There are some jobs that they just don't do. And employees know it.

The truth is, good work is about teamwork. Point the way; lead the group; by being a team player who is willing to pitch in and do whatever is needed, when it is needed. As you rub shoulders with your coworkers, your example will start to rub off on them.

This leader isn't content to just squeak by.

TEACHING THE MOUSE TO ROAR

Think the actions of one leader can't make a difference? Think again. Dee Hansford, who headed Disney World's employee-recognition program in the mid-'90s, was known to spontaneously appear throughout the park to give recognition. She would walk through the kitchen of a restaurant at the theme park and comment on how it sparkled and how Disney's rating with the health board would go through the roof.

In that year, 1995, with no additional employees hired, cast members handled 15 percent more guests at the theme park, received no pay increases or bonuses and still increased their job satisfaction by 15 percentage points.

Guest satisfaction and "interest-to-return" survey scores also were "incredibly high." Moreover, Disney's annual report showed a 15 percent increase in revenues directly attributed to the theme park that year.

THE MORAL: Find the good in what your people are doing and good profits will find you!

Presentation is everything.

PRESENTING FORMAL AWARDS WITH STYLE

Most formal awards are presented without much fanfare. But, according to a survey of 33,000 award recipients, how you present an award makes a significant impression. In fact, 97 percent of employees felt their "contributions were acknowledged" after an "excellent" award presentation, while only 39 percent felt their contributions were acknowledged after a "poor" presentation or no presentation.

Over the next five days, our entries in this book will provide advice on making excellent award presentations.

Choose the right person to present an award.

PRESENTING FORMAL AWARDS WITH STYLE

It's important that the right person make the presentation. And chances are, it's you.

Too often, managers want to invite their boss to make the presentation. After all, the higher ranking the officer the better. Right? Not always. Too often, the CEO fumbles when he tries to pronounce the recipient's name or doesn't know anything about the person's specific accomplishments.

To ensure sincerity and meaning, the presenter of the award should be the highest-ranking manager who personally knows the employee and his or her accomplishments. The person must also be able to evoke emotion — whether with laughter or tears — through anecdotes or examples. For recognition to work, it must evoke feeling in the recipient, in coworkers and in the presenter.

We've got more presentation tips at **www.carrotbooks.com.**

continued ⇨

Prepare in advance.

PRESENTING FORMAL AWARDS WITH STYLE

continuation

As you prepare to make a formal award presentation, make some notes of exactly what is being recognized and be prepared to talk about the employee's specific contributions that have affected the company.

Remember, an award presentation is a time for carrots, not sour grapes. Make only positive, upbeat comments — focusing on the very best things that are happening in your workplace and how the recipient fits into those achievements.

Of course, be careful not to promise continuing employment, not to tell off-color jokes and not to make discriminatory remarks.

continued ⇨

Invite others to attend, and participate.

PRESENTING FORMAL AWARDS WITH STYLE

continuation

Next, to enhance the formal award celebration, invite the employee's colleagues to attend the presentation and ask two or three coworkers to comment on the recipient. Inviting others to participate helps coworkers better appreciate the performance being honored, helps them more clearly understand company goals and helps them emulate successful behavior.

continued ⇨

Invite the recipient to speak.

PRESENTING FORMAL AWARDS WITH STYLE

continuation

During the formal award presentation, allow the recipient to make a few comments. Not everyone will want this opportunity, but every recipient should be asked. This gives the employee a chance to thank others who have helped along the way, to thank those who participated in the recognition experience, and to provide direction to others in attendance who wish to achieve similar results.

continued ⇨

Close with thanks.

PRESENTING FORMAL AWARDS WITH STYLE

continuation

As you conclude the award presentation, offer a sincere thank-you to the employee and a warm handshake.

In all, a great award presentation need not take more than ten or fifteen minutes. But few events are as memorable for employees — those being honored and those watching.

As one CEO confided to us, "Unlike the speeches I give where employees look at me with vacant expressions, no one tunes out in an award presentation." He said speaking at award presentations was the best way for him to reinforce what mattered to the organization, at a time when everyone was engaged and in a celebratory mood.

Give them the star treatment.

A STAR IS BORN

Give an employee with heavenly results a fitting reward: name a star after him. It's easy to do.

To enhance the presentation, consider awarding it at an evening event and attach the registry certificate to a telescope.

"There is a fountain of youth:
It is your talents, the creativity you bring to your life and
the lives of the people you love. When you learn
to tap this source you will truly have defeated age."

— *Sophia Loren, actress*

DRINK DEEPLY

You've seen it on some of your coworkers' faces. It's the look of resignation. They have surrendered to the status quo and no longer believe they can make a difference.

They have gotten old before their time. They have given up.

Lucky for you, you've discovered the fountain of youth: recognition. When you apply your talents and creativity to nurture and build those around you, it refills your cup of enthusiasm and innovative instincts.

So go ahead and quench their thirst for recognition. Drink deeply of life — and you'll never grow old.

Recognition must be positive.

I'D LIKE YOUR AWARD BACK, PLEASE

There are times when employees need praise and recognition. And, of course, there are occasional times when we need to discipline an employee.

However, the two should not be combined.

One well-meaning manager approached us after we gave a talk at a hospital in Texas. She said she gave her employees a handful of tokens at the beginning of the year, and the employees could earn more tokens if they did good things. In December, they could trade them for awards.

"That's a good start," we said.

"And if they make a mistake, I take a token back," she added.

"Yikes," we couldn't help saying out loud.

Cringing, we respectfully suggested she separate her reward and punishment systems. After all, rewards are not something that can be taken back by a mistake.

"There is someone at work who encourages my development."

— *No. 6 on The Gallup Organization's List*
of the Consistent Dimensions of Quality Workplaces

GIVE THE GIFT THAT KEEPS ON GIVING

Most of the time, giving a gift that will benefit yourself is a definite no-no. Like a husband giving his wife season football tickets. Or a drill press. Or (possibly worse) a treadmill.

But there is one exception: when giving an employee award for above-and-beyond performance, consider offering the chance to attend a training seminar. The employee enjoys time to enhance her personal skills (sometimes while visiting another city), and the company benefits from the application of those skills when the employee returns.

Recent research by The Gallup Organization clearly illustrates the connection between employee development and companies with high levels of employee retention, customer satisfaction, productivity and profitability. In fact, "There is someone at work who encourages my development," comes in number six on a list of twelve indicators of a quality workplace with higher customer satisfaction and employee retention.

Think about it. By encouraging employees to develop new skills and knowledge — and providing development resources – you encourage their best efforts.

Tie accomplishment to a symbol.

STANDING FOR SOMETHING

Invent a symbol that represents what you want to be or accomplish in your organization or team. One organization we worked with used a rowboat with several athletes in motion as its symbol. The boat symbolized teamwork, which they wished to stress. This organization presented team members with a rowboat lapel pin when they had served on a number of cross-functional teams, or performed an act of teamwork heroism.

A wearable symbol shows those around that the person has achieved an important milestone and is living one of the core values.

Save the best for last.

THE GRAND FINALE

Develop a year-end award for those in your department who have gone above and beyond on a consistent basis. Make sure you let everyone know this will happen every year, and then follow through.

Get dressed up, and in a formal setting, present your winners with tangible awards that they will value, and offer specific praise. Like the Academy Awards, it'll get bigger and better every year — creating a tradition of excellence and gratitude.

Post the praise.

MAKE NOTE OF IT

Put up a bulletin board in your department and post letters of praise from internal and external customers. Write your own handwritten notes of thanks and congratulations on the bottom of the letters, letting your people know what they do doesn't go unnoticed by clients or by you.

Believe in the possibilities.

THEN BREAK RECORDS

You know the story. Before 1954, medical experts believed that it was humanly impossible to run a mile in less than four minutes. After all, in the entire history of mankind, no one had ever done it. Then, on May 6, 1954, Roger Bannister crossed the mile marker in 3:59.4 minutes and everything changed. In following years, dozens of other athletes would literally follow in Banner's footsteps to break the four-minute mile.

What made the difference? Did their fitness level drastically rise? More likely, their sights did. They had seen it done. They believed they could do it — and so did the rest of the world.

Employees aren't much different from those runners. They need managers who believe in them — and regularly tell them so. If a manager is convinced that the people in her group are first rate — and she regularly expresses this belief through recognition — they'll reliably outperform a group whose manager believes the reverse, even if the innate talent of the two groups is similar.

Let him help in the hiring process.

GET TECHNICAL

Ask a high performer to assist in the hiring process by conducting technical interviews (to verify job skills). It demonstrates a high level of trust and confidence in the employee — as well as builds leadership skills.

Put an incredible performer in his place.

FIRST CLASS

When an outstanding employee is facing a particularly long business flight, upgrade him to business or first class. He'll feel so good, his feet won't even touch the ground.

Where along the way did things go wrong?

RETRACING OUR STEPS

Somewhere along the way, we got way off track. We began to see management as the ability to crunch numbers and facilitate meetings and compose flow charts. Businesses began to expend billions of dollars each year on executive training, much of it heavily focused on leadership skills.

Ironically, evidence has emerged that these types of "quantitative" executive training expenditures yield very low rates of return on investment for their corporate sponsors. Some experts estimate that the return on investment from these costs may be as low as 10 percent.

In our minds — and those of many others — leadership is the natural outcome of a sincere relationship of mutual respect between employees and supervisors. A relationship that includes regular, sincere recognition.

"Play it for me, Sam."

— *Humphrey Bogart, actor, in* Casablanca

ENCORE! ENCORE!

When things are flowing along smoothly; when people are working in concert — those are the times to applaud their efforts with recognition. Chances are, they'll give you an encore performance.

We'll never forget the words of an employee in the operations division of a major investment management company who had just received an exceptional achievement award for assuming double duty while his boss was out on a five-month maternity leave.

He said, "People in management at most companies probably don't realize how the worker bees feel about their jobs day to day. It means so much to us if they take the time to recognize us — whether through a formal program or just a verbal 'good job' now and then."

The employee paused and we asked him, "Would you do this type of action again?" He nodded. "After the kind of recognition I got today, you bet I'd do it again."

Getting the job done.

A LITTLE FRIENDLY COMPETITION

Given the number of clichés they use in interviews, we've decided all professional athletes must have the same media coach. How often have you heard one of them say, "We just focus on one game at a time."

It's good for a laugh . . . and, when you think of it, for your employees.

A little healthy competition between stores or divisions can help employees focus on the job at hand — and then some. Consider creating a trophy that travels to the store or team that had the best results for a month or quarter. It will get people's hearts pumping and the ball rolling.

Haven't I seen you someplace before?

FACE TIME

After her first day of high school, our friend's little sister came home with a knowing smile. She couldn't wait to tell everyone she'd seen a picture of Kelly (our friend) mounted on the school wall — sporting the requisite Farrah Fawcett hair of the 1980s. As it turns out, Kelly had been a student body officer in 1985, something she was proud of then — and now.

Of course, her sister thought the hair was hilarious. Kelly's reaction was a little different. She was surprised — and (to be honest) a little bit flattered. She'd had no idea her long-ago accomplishment was still on display.

In hopes of creating that same reaction, many companies have Walks of Fame, displaying pictures of employees who have been recently rewarded for outstanding performance or length of service.

These walks serve as a highly visible — and lasting — reminder of an employee's accomplishment.

We're all on the same side.

NOT SO DIFFERENT AT ALL

Do you ever feel pulled in three different directions? Needing to keep customers happy ... and investors ... and employees.

No sweat. You can pull it all together — by simply changing your mind-set.

During the 1990s, conventional wisdom told us that customers, investors and employees were three different animals. In fact, we were taught that they were mutually exclusive. To please one, you must, of necessity, shortcut the other.

Nothing could be farther from the truth. When employees are happy, you get happy customers. And happy, loyal customers return again and again, generating greater profits — which can't help but make investors very, very happy.

REMEMBER: When employees are happy, everyone's happy.

*"Appreciative words are the
most powerful force for good on earth!"*

— *George W. Crane, publisher*

WELL, THAT WAS EASY!

One of the most common things we hear from supervisors about recognition is that it just seems too simple to work. And we have to agree — to a point.

Of course, you have to get through the learning curve, which can be difficult. But once a person becomes comfortable giving recognition, it is just about the easiest, most natural thing you'll ever do — with shockingly big results!

Recognition. It seems a little thing; but sometimes the little things can mean the most. (And this is one of those times.)

Got a task that seems overwhelming? Let recognition cut it down to size.

MISSION POSSIBLE

What do 1,600 pounds of chicken wings have to do with recognition? Everything, if you talk to Mary Cadagin.

We first heard of this exceptional leader two years ago, when she spear headed her organization's data center move. Her team included 550 employees who had been asked to work their day jobs all week and then spend 13 consecutive weekends (including Friday all-nighters) to move the center — all without the promise of extra pay.

Part of the secret was food. Friday nights were kicked off with themed dinners. Chicken wings were part of the regular midnight snacks. And Saturday morning meant full-on breakfasts of pancakes, eggs and bacon.

But there was more. Mary showed concern for her workers, providing overnight hotel stays for those too tired to drive home. She had a sense of humor, holding *Hill Street Blues*-type meetings before the weekend kicked into high gear. And she was constantly present during the move, giving thanks and encouragement.

When the project was completed, she convinced the company to hand out bonuses to all employees involved in the relocation — and threw a picnic for them and their families.

That's the power of a leader who understands the power of recognition.

SEPTEMBER

*"At the end of your life, you are going to want to know
that you made some kind of difference."*

— *Susan Sarandon, actress*

PUT THEM IN THE KNOW

Assumptions can get you into trouble. Like assuming that employees know they are making a difference without you telling them. The truth is, they probably don't know. And they most likely won't. Until you tell them. And they shouldn't have to wait until the end of their work lives to hear it. The sooner you tell them, the better.

Today, find someone making a difference where you work and let her know how her work is contributing to the success of your department.

The Dirty Dozen of Why We Don't

EXCUSE NO. 9

"THEY'LL ASK FOR MORE MONEY."

Actually, no, they don't! In fact, quite the opposite! Research shows that people who are paid fairly and receive recognition ask for fewer salary increases. (Go figure, huh?) That's because they're not looking for a reason to stay. They've already found it. (And it didn't cost you much, either.) Keep people happy and engaged and they are less likely to complain about money. It's a fact!

Enhance the award with your company logo.

GIVE IT TROPHY VALUE

A recent survey shows that when an award includes a quality emblem or symbol, or features an engraved message, it gains "trophy value" that cannot be matched in any other way — not with cash, not with gift certificates, not with trips and not with merchandise alone.

The survey of 17,000 recognition award recipients showed that 74 percent of employees who receive awards featuring their corporate symbol feel the symbol enhances the meaning of their award.

An item with a logo — or an award that's personalized — reminds the recipient that it was earned, and that it couldn't have been purchased.

> *"You have to treat your employees like your customers.*
> *When you treat them right,*
> *they will treat your outside customers right."*

> — *Herb Kelleher, former CEO, Southwest Airlines*

TREAT THEM RIGHT

You treat your customers right — right? You're polite. You make sure they have a good experience at your business. You try to meet their needs. You treat them like they matter.

And that, it turns out, is the same way you should treat your employees.

Contrary to popular belief, treating an employee as a customer doesn't mean you give him a free ride — it means you respect him and assist him in meeting his goals.

As F. Robert Salerno, Avis president, put it, "At Avis, where we famously 'try harder' for customers, we have formalized a way for our managers to recognize and reward their people. We do it because we see a true 'value chain' through which motivated employees become more likely to motivate customer loyalty."

Go ahead, treat employees right. They'll treat your customers to an amazing level of customer service.

> *"One of the most effective ways*
> *to motivate known to man*
> *is one of the most simple: a compliment."*

— *Adrian Gostick and Chester Elton, authors*

SINCERELY, YOUR BOSS

The truth, and nothing but the truth. That's the golden rule for giving compliments. (And, as it happens, it works well in the courtroom, too.)

You should never feel the need to embellish an employee's accomplishment or exaggerate their impact. When giving a compliment, simply say what you mean and mean what you say. If you don't, it will show and your good intentions will be wasted.

Of course, sincerity comes most naturally when complimenting behaviors that truly advance company goals. Be on the lookout for those types of activities. When you've found one, go ahead and tell the employee the truth — that their actions make the company a success. And you're grateful.

Time for a story about recognition.

JUST "WATCH" TURNOVER RATES FALL

On an employee's 25th service anniversary with Avis, the company presents him or her with a Rolex watch. It is among the many reasons that an amazing 10 percent of Avis employees have been with the company for at least twenty years.

Says F. Robert Salerno, Avis president, "Beyond it being, I believe, a generous gesture, it also serves as a symbol of the reliability of both our employees and our rental car operations."

*"You don't have to be a fantastic hero to do certain things —
to compete. You can be just an ordinary chap,
sufficiently motivated to reach challenging goals."*

— *Sir Edmund Hillary, first climber to summit Mt. Everest*

BE THE MOTIVATOR

We all have stars in our organizations and we count on them to achieve. But the fact is that our "B" players can also have great impact — if they are motivated.

In a *USA Today* article, here is what writer Del Jones has to say about the role of "B" players: "The importance of B players may be only now dawning on the experts, but it's one of those common-sense discoveries that many garden-variety workers have subscribed to all along. The backbone of every company is in the middle where the ether of great thoughts is hammered into reality."

Every boss knows the frustration of seeing great ideas fall through the cracks. In their best-selling business book, *Execution: The Discipline of Getting Things Done,* coauthors Larry Bossidy and Ram Charan argue that the biggest obstacle to success is not a lack of grand vision, but turning a little vision into some product, service or useful innovation.

"B players are crucial," says Bossidy, retired CEO of Honeywell. "They may get directions from others, but they're the ones who execute."

*"There are two things employees want more than
sex and money: recognition and praise."*

—*Mary Kay Ash, founder, Mary Kay Cosmetics*

GIVE THE PEOPLE WHAT THEY WANT

Admit it. Reading this quote, there's a tiny part of you still struggling to believe employees would really and truly choose recognition over money . . . or the other thing.

So did the Public Radio International talk-show host who interviewed us several years ago, shortly after the release of our first book, *Managing With Carrots*. Still skeptical, even after the wisdom we imparted during our interview, he decided to put recognition to the test. He tried a few of the ideas from the book on his office staff and then asked several people in his office (a very scientific survey) if they would want a job that paid loads and loads of money, or one where they felt appreciated and rewarded.

To his utter dismay, every single person in his office chose recognition over cash. He had to admit on air, "Managing with carrots. It works!"

But, then, we already knew that.

Trying to find a way to keep your top employees?

IT'S JUST DOWN THE HALL

Cynthia Stotlar, president of the Society for Human Resource Management, tells the story of a manager within a hospital plagued by 60 percent turnover company wide. Except in the laundry. The manager there reported just 5 percent turnover.

His employees worked a hot, difficult job for just above minimum wage. How did he do it? Recognition. He built a "Hall of Fame." Each time an employee went above and beyond, he put up an 8 x 10 glossy of the employee, along with a paragraph telling what they did to earn the award.

Similar success stories follow managers' conversions to recognition. Their employees' performance skyrockets, and the process is never ending. It has a viruslike effect on an organization. As managers' expectations of employees rise and recognition of their work follows, so does employee performance.

(Want to really clean up around the office? The key is recognition.)

"I can live two months on a good compliment."

— *Mark Twain, author*

SOMETHING TO HOLD ONTO

We were once told by an enlightened manager, "You know, I've discovered you really don't need to provide recognition very often. Just during the weeks you eat."

He's right, you know. Food keeps our bodies alive. Recognition feeds our egos, minds and souls. It's what keeps us going, trying and achieving. As a manager, you should be recognizing someone with some form of recognition every week.

REMEMBER: For a strong and healthy organization, feed employees a steady diet of recognition.

A day of tragedy brings out employee heroes.

IN THE LINE OF DUTY

Recognition is all about employees like Shawn Smith and Robert Djulus, shuttlers in Avis's Toronto, Canada, location. They earned Horizon awards when, in the wake of September 11, they helped an elderly couple who returned their car and were trying to get back home.

Once the couple realized they were not going to be able to get a flight or hotel room, they were prepared to sleep in the airport. When the couple shared this story with Shawn and Robert, both men offered their homes to the customers. Ultimately, Shawn drove the couple to his home that evening and made arrangements for them during the course of the following day for hotel and airline flights as soon as possible.

Both Shawn and Robert showed superb customer service skills and compassion during that difficult time. Said F. Robert Salerno, Avis president, "They certainly showed the 'We try harder "spirit."

Set her spirits soaring.

SEND A BALLOON BOUQUET

Send a balloon bouquet to a great employee to recognize her for above-and-beyond achievement. If you're feeling particularly light-hearted, take a hit of helium before you express your gratitude.

Try a different "type" of recognition.

AN ELECTRIC THANK-YOU

Today, send e-mails of thanks to three employees. Mention their roles in a recent project and how much you appreciate their contributions.

Guaranteed, you'll get three heartfelt thank-yous in return.

> *"Outstanding leaders go out of their way to boost the*
> *self-esteem of their personnel.*
> *If people believe in themselves, it is amazing*
> *what they can accomplish."*

— *Sam Walton, former CEO, Wal-Mart*

A LEG UP

Have you ever noticed the common theme running through superhero movies? Before Spiderman or Superman or the Incredible Hulk can accomplish anything, they have to believe in themselves and their purpose.

And so do your employees. You have a responsibility for a group of people who will spend a large part of their lives at work. They need to find the areas where they excel. They need to believe that they have the skills and ability to do their jobs well.

Recognition enhances employee self-esteem and empowers them to achieve. Who knows? They may even find ways to do things no one has ever done before. (Sounds a little like a superhero to us.)

Recognition always gets a warm reception.

THE FIRST PERSON YOU SEE

Surprise the receptionist at work with donuts or a simple thank-you card and watch as the reception area becomes brighter and friendlier.

Chances are that few people thank this individual — the person who most customers view as the face of your company.

Give teenage workers flexibility to
attend important school events.

TIME OUT!

Often, the best reward you can give part-time teenage workers is
flexibility in their schedules — to attend band camp in the summer,
a football game in the fall, or a night off with friends anytime.

"You like me, you really like me!"

— *Sally Fields, actress*

WHAT THEY DON'T KNOW . . .

Some people don't know that they are appreciated until you tell them. There are Sally Fields all over you organization doing good work in obscurity. Find them and tell them you like them!

Bring the group together to announce promotions.

PROMOTE TEAM LOYALTY

Bring your entire team together to announce promotions. Many managers are afraid of jealousy if they do this; but the news gets out anyway. Give the person his well-deserved moment in the sun. If you've been fostering the right feelings among the others, they'll be content to offer their praise, too.

Whittle while she works.

SHORTEN HER TO-DO LIST

Show a truly reliable employee how much their dedication means: hire a concierge service for a week to whittle down her to-do list. Such services will shop for gifts, find estimates for repair work, book dinner or flight reservations, return books to the library, and pick up groceries. You name it, they probably can do it. Come to think of it, that sounds a lot like your employee, huh?

"It is not enough to merely believe in recognition.
You also have to BEHAVE like you believe in it!"

— *Eric Harvey, author*

I SPY

Someone is watching you. In fact, every one of your employees is watching you.

"So many of us who are leaders believe that we're invisible, that we can walk through the organization and no one will know," Bob Rosner, a syndicated columnist told *The Business Journal of Central New York*. "Your people watch you, talk about you, study you. They have a Ph.D. in you."

That's why it's so important that your walk "is in sync with your talk," says Rosner.

CHALLENGE: Think of ways your actions contradict your professed belief in recognition. Set specific goals to bring the two into closer alignment.

They said there was nothing employees could do about it.

PROVING THEM WRONG

Inspiring leaders can get employees to do incredible things. We love the true story about Ralph Harding, former manager of General Motors' Wilmington, Delaware, plant. In the early 1990s, executives from headquarters gathered the plant's 3,500 workers to tell them their factory would be closed by 2006. "There is nothing you can do to affect this decision," they were told by the visiting GM suits.

After the executives left, Harding made an impassioned speech to the shell-shocked workers. "There may be nothing we can do to affect the decision," Harding said, "But there is something we *can* do: we can make them feel really stupid! Because they are going to be closing the best plant in General Motors!"

Within two years, the workers made the factory the lowest-cost producer in GM, with the lowest warranty costs as well. Car dealers began specifically requesting Chevy Corsicas and Berretta models made by the Wilmington plant. GM reversed itself in 1996 and kept the plant open.

"They didn't expect financial rewards," recalls Harvey G. Thomas, the plant's current manager. "It was their [the employees'] sense of self-esteem more than anything else. Nobody wants to walk out of a closed plant."

Ahhh! That's just what I needed!

MADE-TO-ORDER RECOGNITION

One CPA firm believes employee rewards can keep employees satisfied and committed, even when they are working hard. That's why the fifty-person firm adopted stress relievers ranging from in-office back massages to giving employees every other Friday off in the summer.

Not only that, but employees who go above and beyond and work on Saturdays are supplied with catered full-course luncheons. And lunch is not restricted to the employees; spouses and children sometimes join them.

The firm's human resources coordinator says whenever she senses a stressful situation in the office, she goes to a nearby Dairy Queen, gets Dilly Bars, and then walks around to everyone's desk offering a choice of flavors.

The early bird gets the worm.

YOU SNOOZE, EVERYONE LOSES

Some leaders who have tried recognition complain that one or two of their people think they are insincere. Upon investigation, we often find that the way recognition is handled is a large part of the problem.

In one case, a manager complained about an employee publicly praising herself before he could do it and then being suspicious of her manager's later praise. We taught the manager to make recognition events more timely and to add specific praise with stories. Remarkably, the problem soon evaporated.

Find out how you are doing.

ASK FOR FEEDBACK

There are some things you'd probably rather not know. But go ahead and ask anyway.

To show your employees that you are trying to recognize and reward their behaviors, take a deep breath and ask them how you are doing in this regard. Encourage them to be honest. And, most importantly, accept the feedback — good or bad — with nothing more (or less) than thanks.

> ***"The highest compliments leaders can receive
> are those that are given by people that work for them."***
>
> — *James L. Barksdale, businessman*

DO THEY COMPLIMENT YOU?

In the movie *Field of Dreams,* a farmer repeatedly hears a voice urging him to turn his field of corn into a baseball field. "If you build it, they will come," it says.

And they did.

It's the same with supervisors who regularly receive compliments from the people who work for them. First they had to build a culture of recognition (and correct any areas where they were mismanaging staff) — and the compliments just naturally followed.

WARNING: If you haven't received any compliments for a while, that's a message in and of itself. Take some time out to examine your management style and correct areas that need improvement. Then set the example by recognizing others.

Create a management style worthy of praise — and it will come.

Notice the nuances.

APPRECIATING TALENT

The story goes that a tourist once spotted Pablo Picasso sketching in a Paris cafe and asked if he would sketch her. She offered to pay him fair value. In just a few minutes, Picasso had finished. When asked what she owed him, Picasso asked for the large sum of 5,000 francs.

"But it only took you a few minutes," protested the tourist.

"No," said Picasso, "it took me my whole life."

Sometimes, as supervisors, we take for granted the knowledge and skill base of our workers — because they make their jobs look easy. It's not until they have left the company for greener pastures and we try to find someone with similar qualifications that we truly appreciate what we had.

What unique abilities, knowledge and experiences do each of your employees bring to the table, benefiting the company each day? Appreciating these often-overlooked nuances shows a sharp eye and an appreciation for talent — the mark of a master at recognition.

We're all in this together. Or are we?

SPEAKING IN THIRD PERSON

Are the pronouns your employees use pro-company?

The words employees use when speaking of the company can be an indicator of how they feel. If they choose inclusive words like "us" and "we," then they feel a connection to the company. But if they speak of the company in third person, using terms such as "they" or "them," there's a definite disconnect — and you need to find a way to rebuild the relationship.

"Being cheerful keeps you happy."

— *King Solomon, ancient Babylonian leader*

MAKE YOUR MIND UP

Happiness isn't something that one can be given. It isn't something that arrives one day, like a package, when the conditions are just right. It's a choice. It's a decision.

So it's ironic that so many managers — who are paid to make the big decisions — can't seem to make up their minds to simply be positive.

Today, make a goal to remain unruffled no matter what happens around you. When people ask you, "How's it going?" answer, "If it gets any better, it wouldn't be fair!" As you adopt a cheerful, positive attitude, you will feel happier in your job. And so will your employees.

Send recognition via snail mail.

SPECIAL DELIVERY!

A truly gracious gesture is to send a care package to an employee's child attending college away from home. This is particularly appreciated around stressful exam times — recognizing the young person for making it through a semester of hard work.

You can make your own gift box stuffed with fast food gift certificates, movie passes, school supplies, stamps and goodies. Or order one on-line from one of the many companies that offer such packages. You'll get high marks for thoughtfulness.

"Many times, the difference between your accomplishment and your failure is your attitude."

— *Author unknown*

TURN IT AROUND

A wise saying goes like this: "Experience comes from good judgment; but good judgment comes from bad experience."

Everyone makes mistakes sometimes — even the boss. Turn yours into team-building moments by admitting your error to colleagues and brainstorming ways to avoid the mistake going forward.

The approach has many benefits: (1) Employees will be impressed by your candidness and honesty; (2) they will be prepared to avoid the same mistake themselves; (3) they will feel safer admitting mistakes to you in the future (rather than trying to cover them up); and (4) they will feel freer to be innovative.

OCTOBER

*"Giving frees us from the familiar territory
of our own needs by opening our minds to the unexplored
worlds occupied by the needs of others."*

— *Barbara Bush, former U.S. first lady*

TAKE ME TO YOUR LEADER

No doubt about it, recognition moves you into alien territory — a.k.a. your employees' world. And from where they sit, everything looks a whole lot different.

We've discovered that the more you give of yourself in learning about your employees (their needs, their likes, their dislikes), the more your perspective changes and you find yourself better able to lead them — with compassion, understanding, and confidence (because you know them and you know they'll follow).

After a while, you may ask yourself why you never saw all this before. It's because (and we mean this kindly) you've been on another planet. We're glad you're back.

The Dirty Dozen of Why We Don't

EXCUSE NO. 10

"NO ONE ELSE AROUND HERE DOES IT."

Hey, if no one else around here jumped off a cliff, would you not jump either? Wait, that's not right.

Anyway, the point is, you'll stand out all the more if you recognize! Being innovative and leading out gives you an opportunity to shine. Lead out today and let the sheep follow behind!

Like day and night.

SEEING THE LIGHT

Barbara Ruddy had worked at the Arizona Department of Economic Security for thirty years when we met her. During the course of our conversation, she told us her five- and ten-year service awards had arrived impersonally in the mail. Her fifteen-year award arrived an amazing three years late, because her boss couldn't be bothered to fill out the paperwork.

But her twenty-year service award was different. Her new boss gathered colleagues. He delved into her personnel file and told the group every job Barbara had held in the department for the last two decades. "Near the end," said Barbara, "he thanked me for all I had brought to the department. I had tears in my eyes. No one had ever recognized me in front of my peers before."

Barbara was so moved by this simple presentation, she asked to take over the department's recognition program so she could teach managers how to make effective service-award presentations that would have an emotional impact on employees and bond them to their organization.

> *"Of all the things you wear,
> your expression is the most important."*
>
> — *Janet Lane, actress*

FACE LIFT

You can see it in their faces. When people are recognized, they feel great about themselves and the people they work with. Watch how expressions change when you recognize someone for a job well done today. We bet you won't be able to stop smiling, either.

Stop them dead in their tracks.

MAKE A U-TURN

In a survey by the Nierenberg Group, working professionals were asked what would make them reconsider staying at a job they planned to leave. They responded:

- More opportunities for advancement
- Increase in salary and benefits
- Better recognition for contributions

Since you don't have much control over one and two, if you're looking for a way to turn things around, recognition is it!

*"The change of viewing employees as an asset
or a source of revenue production rather than a cost
is a whole mind shift for the business community.
People are coming to grips with the fact that you make your
numbers because of the people you employ."*

— *James E. Copeland, Jr., CEO, Deloitte Touche Tohmatsu*

GOT GOOD PEOPLE?

Do you remember watching *A Team,* a formulaic "dramedy" about a group of ex-cons turned vigilante detective agency? Every episode would wind up with the A Team facing certain destruction. Then the mechanical genius of the group would miraculously pull together an incredible device (vehicle, weapon, whatever) out of dental floss and scotch tape — and annihilate the enemy. We loved every minute of it.

THE MORAL: You can't keep a good team down.

The ability of human beings to rally behind a cause and turn things around is legendary. If you are going to get out of a hole, your people are the ones who will do it for you. Likewise, when you are on top of your industry, it's your people who put you there.

Recognition skills are not something you're born with.

GET IN TRAINING

There is an art to giving compliments. That's why we encourage all the managers we meet with to go to recognition training. Don't think you need it? Here's just one example of how easily recognition can go wrong.

The goal, in this example, is to give specific, positive recognition. Something along the lines of: "Bill, I'm really pleased with the way you coordinated the task force meeting. As you know, cost containment is a key goal of our company this year, and you and your group came up with a very practical yet creative solution to our problem that helps meet that goal. The savings will be more than $10,000 to our department. Fantastic work."

Without training, the message might instead come out nonspecific and broad, like this: "Bill, many thanks for all the work you did this past year. You're really a terrific person. I really like knowing you." (Add "Have a great summer, let's do stuff" and you'd have a yearbook message.)

Or, even worse, the praise may be tinged with negative messages: "Bill, I thought you presented some great ideas this morning. Those folks really took note of your suggestions. I'm not happy, however, with the way you handled the group. You never drew them out. . . ."

Knowledge is power. The short time you spend in recognition training will pay dividends for years to come.

> *"Generally, appreciation means some blend of thankfulness, admiration, approval, and gratitude. In the financial world, something that 'appreciates' grows in value. With the power tool of appreciation, you get the benefit of both perspectives."*

— *Doc Childre and Howard Martin, The HeartMath Solution*

LET IT APPRECIATE

Did you know your recognition efforts could be "appreciating" faster than your money market fund? It's true.

The Watson Wyatt Human Capital Index shows that clear rewards and accountability generate 16.5 to 21.5 percent growth in annual shareholder value, as well as 5.4 to 14.6 percent improvement in recruitment and retention.

They'll gobble up this reward.

GIVE THANKS

Thanksgiving is the perfect time to express your gratitude to your staff. (That's why we're telling you this early . . . even before Canadian Thanksgiving . . . so you have time to prepare.)

This year, send a box of chocolates to each employee's home, along with a note of gratitude. It's thoughtful. It's classy. (And it shouldn't replace your Christmas gift.)

While we're on the subject, sending a small food gift home once in a while is a nice touch. Who wouldn't love a fresh strawberry pie or cherry cheesecake delivered to their door in the summer? Little extra touches like these remind employees of your respect and regard — and build the same feelings within the employee for you.

> *"People expect me, as the CEO,*
> *to talk about innovation and operating excellence*
> *and client care, our corporate capabilities.*
> *But I could talk until I'm blue in the face*
> *and it wouldn't be as impactful as when employees talk about*
> *these values during a service-award presentation."*

— *Kent Murdock, CEO, O. C. Tanner*

A PERFECT ILLUSTRATION

Remember the buddy system? It teaches us to never go it alone. On the mountain, this rule saves lives. In the office, it saves companies.

Through recognition, employees share the burden of spreading your company's mission, vision and values throughout the organization. They illustrate the company brand, vision, values and strategy through their every-day activities and priorities. They live it. They embrace it. And they teach it to each other through example.

So you don't have to do it all alone.

And that's an incredible benefit, because second only to their direct super-visor, employees most value recognition and direction from their peers.

Recognize. Because the company you save may be your own.

Sometimes the best reward is when the boss gets dirty.

DO THEIR LEAST FAVORITE TASK

After we spoke in Las Vegas to a group of managers from a water-conditioning company, one leader approached us. He told us that when his people hit a safety goal — making so many deliveries without accident or injury — they get to be boss for the day, sit in the air-conditioned office and answer the phone — while the general manager makes their deliveries. And in Las Vegas, when you make deliveries in 120-degree heat, that means a lot.

His employees would walk through fire for their manager. And he walks through the hot-as-fire desert for them.

*"I think the biggest disease
the world suffers from in this day and age
is the disease of people feeling unloved."*

— *Princess Diana, princess of Wales*

Ingratitude is a disease. And it's killing American companies. Fortunately, there is a cure — a simple "thank you." Inoculate your staff today.

Keep spending under control.

JUST MAKES CENTS

L et's talk dollars and cents for a moment, because recognition can save you a lot of them.

There is a benefit to gifts in kind (non-cash rewards) that many supervisors overlook. That is, they are non-negotiable. While cash awards, which employees may want to see consolidated into their pay raises, can cause wage bills to creep up without any corresponding rise in productivity, non-cash benefits hold no such dangers.

When you think about it that way, non-cash awards just makes cents.

Spin the wheel, win a prize!

GET IN THE GAME

An electronics company believes in keeping employees in the game — literally.

Supervisors give employees stickers or certificates in recognition for a job well done. Employees who collect four or more are eligible to play "the game" at the next monthly employee meeting.

The game varies each month (roulette wheel, bowling, fishing, etc.) and employees can win a simple prize, usually valued at $5 to $7.

The game doesn't cost very much, and that's just the point, says their director of general affairs. "The purpose of rewards and recognition is not to compensate employees for their extra effort on the job; it is a small token for a large amount of thanks and gratitude."

Give them a brush with fame.

"THE KING" OF REWARDS

Arrange for an employee's favorite local celebrity to pay them an on-the-job visit and present an award. (Or hire an actor to impersonate their favorite star — living or dead. This is great if you have an Elvis or Marilyn Monroe fan on your staff.) Take photos and frame them for a follow-up award presentation.

*"When a happy person comes into the room,
it is as if another candle has been lit."*

— *Ralph Waldo Emerson, poet*

IF YOU'RE HAPPY AND YOU KNOW IT . . .

Have you ever met a person who brightens a room . . . by leaving it? Sounds like someone who hasn't discovered the power of recognition.

Recognition is all about positive feelings and being happy at work. Start with your own attitude and be the light that enters the room.

Like they say, you take the party with you. So, what are you waiting for? Let the celebration begin!

It happens only once a year.

THE TOP 10

Get rid of Employee of the Year programs. They benefit only one person, and that person typically feels embarrassed to be singled out.

Instead, give out Presidential Awards or Chairman's Awards to the top ten or twenty employees in your company. This type of recognition should include a tangible, keepsake reminder of the accomplishment and a personal meeting with the president or chairman.

Now, instead of one employee, you have gone a long way to identifying and retaining a small army of great performers.

Think they're doing great work? "Show" them!

ON THE BIG SCREEN

The next time a blockbuster movie is released, get matinee tickets for the first day. (Yes, during work hours!) Take your staff to the movie together — and spring for treats.

Some theaters run local advertising before the movie. Increase this reward's impact by buying an ad and thanking them on the big screen.

"It's time for us all to stand and cheer
for the do'er, the achiever —
the one who recognizes the challenge and
does something about it!"

— *Vince Lombardi, Hall of Fame football coach*

CHEER THEM ON

"And so the brave knight returned in triumph to the empty streets of his village. He slopped his pigs and went to bed. No one seemed to care that the village was no longer terrorized by the terrible dragon. So the knight put away his sword and lived a quiet, anonymous life, dying gently in his sleep one winter day."

It's not the kind of ending you anticipate. Certainly not a happy one. But it's exactly the ending you get in a company that lacks recognition programs.

Within these companies, talented and energetic employees are repeatedly overlooked until, disappointed by the lack of reaction to their heroic efforts, they put away their swords and wait out their careers in a half-sleep or move on to more promising territory.

It doesn't have to be that way. The solution lies in employee recognition . . . the modern hero's welcome. Decide today to head the welcome party.

A Car in Every Garage.

PUTTING RECOGNITION INTO HIGH GEAR

A telecommunications company rewards its best employees for their outstanding performance and dedication to success by offering them cars. Through the Car in Every Garage program, honored employees are permitted to choose either a BMW Z3, BMW 325, an Audi TT or a Dodge Durango.

The first cars were awarded to employees who, according to the company, went the distance and then some. In a competitive market for top talent, this program helps the company recruit and keep great people. Employees are eligible to participate in the program after two years with the company. Cars are leased and paid for by the company and given to the employee for a period of three years, with an option to buy at the end of the contract.

*"Gone are the days when people stay
because they love their organization.
Today, great people stay
because they love the people they work for."*

— *Adrian Gostick and Chester Elton, authors*

TIES THAT BIND

This is one case where it really is all about you. (All those other times, well, we really can't say.)

Contrary to popular belief, employees bond to their managers, not to their companies. When a manager is good, so is performance. When he's bad, so goes just about everything else.

In the 2002 Global Employee Commitment Study, 20,000 workers in thirty-three countries were asked for feedback on key management skills associated with highly productive cultures. Employees from high-performance firms consistently rated their managers much higher than those in poorly performing businesses.

Feel that? It's the weight of responsibility. Bear it well.

Got a model employee?

GIVE THEM WHEELS

Is one of your employees a car fanatic? Give him his dream car for a week as a thank-you. Arrange it through a high-end rental company; then take the employee out to sign the final papers and drive it home.

Another variation: give him a high quality model of his favorite vehicle to display in his office. Add to its trophy value by engraving a congratulatory message in the license-plate area.

Have you found her weakness?

MAKE IT HER STRENGTH

Is there a part of your employee's job that she struggles with? Recognition can take that weakness and make it her strength.

According to research conducted at the University of Alberta, rewards can awaken interest, build confidence and beef up performance for activities employees don't enjoy — making cold calls, doing performance appraisals, etc.

"Employees have a knowledge base you can't get anywhere else. Equipment, procedures — those things can be duplicated. When you look at competitive advantage, human capital is the only area where companies can really differentiate themselves."

— *Meldron Young, American Management Association*

A STANDOUT

The other day, we pulled up to a drive-thru to grab a quick lunch on the go. We still shake our heads when remembering what happened next. It went something like this:

"Hi. We'll start with a No. 6 combo meal, supersized, with a Diet Coke."

"Okay, so would you like to supersize that?"

"Yes. We'd like a No. 6 combo meal, supersized, with a Diet Coke."

"So what kind of drink would you like with that?"

After several more similarly frustrating interactions, and with time running short, we finally gave up, pulled to the restaurant next door and whizzed through their drive-thru in nothing flat. Same technology. Same product. Same customer. So what made the difference? The employee.

Employees are your competitive advantage (or disadvantage, as the case may be). Let them know through recognition that they are important and are doing the right things.

This turnover doesn't leave a good taste in your mouth.

TOO EXPENSIVE FOR MY TASTE

You probably know turnover is expensive. You just may not realize how expensive.

Studies calculate the cost to replace an employee is at a bare minimum 30 percent of salary — and can rise to as high as 200 percent. Such calculations take into account advertising costs, temporary replacement costs or overtime costs while the job is vacant, lost opportunity costs, search-firm fees, relocation costs, time to interview, and time and cost to orient and train the new person.

Nowadays, it's not enough to just get good people in your front door. You need to find ways to keep them from walking out the back door. Recognition is the solution.

A Watson-Wyatt Reward Plan Survey of 614 employers with 3.5 million employees demonstrated that the average turnover rate of employers with a clearly articulated reward strategy is 13 percent lower than that of organizations without a well-communicated plan.

Hey, 3.5 million workers can't be wrong. Slow the flow with recognition.

It's only fair.

GETTING EVEN

All's fair in love ... and work. According to Stacy Adams, that could be the mantra of unrecognized workers everywhere.

Adams is the author of the *Equity Theory,* which proposes that once an employee chooses an action that is expected to satisfy his or her needs, the individual assesses the equity, or fairness, of that outcome.

If the employee feels rewarded, they are satisfied and motivated. If the employee feels under-rewarded, he will try one of two approaches: (1) increasing the outcome, or (2) decreasing his input. And, we should tell you, neither is terribly good for business.

To increase the outcome, the employee may:

- Ask for a raise or promotion
- Seek out greater recognition
- Seek new employment

To decrease output, the employee may:

- Become less productive (not work as hard)
- Be absent more frequently
- Cognitively downgrade the skill level or amount of education (not put as much thought into the work)

"Some rank and file are diamonds in the rough.
They just don't know how to navigate the corporate culture or
how to toot their own horns or aggressively forge
their own career paths. . . . There is a need to develop bosses
into coaches so they can spot and develop these diamonds."

— *Lupe Torre, Monfia*

MINING FOR DIAMONDS

It isn't pressure that turns coal into diamonds. It's the right boss.
If you've ever looked around at your staff and wondered, "Why me?" then
it may be time to take a good, long look in the mirror.

Employees are what you make them. It takes a supervisor with a sharp
eye, who isn't afraid to build their people, to spot the diamonds in the
rough and recognize their potential. But they are there, nevertheless ,wait-
ing for the right leader to help them shine.

Be that leader.

Do your employees have a commitment problem?

FITTING THE PROFILE

We found this interesting: The Global Employee Commitment Study shows that successful companies have different employee-commitment profiles than less-successful organizations.

As part of the study, researchers classified employees into the following three categories.

- Ambassadors. Employees who are fully committed to their companies and their work.

- Company-oriented. People who are more dedicated to their employers than to their work or career.

- Career-oriented. Individuals who place their careers over company needs.

- Disengaged workers. Employees who are not committed to their companies or careers.

Top-performing companies proved to have a significantly higher percentage of "Ambassadors" (45 percent) than did poorer performing companies (36 percent). They also had fewer "Career-oriented" employees (14 percent as opposed to 24 percent at poorer performing firms) and fewer "Disengaged" employees (26 percent as opposed to 30 percent).

What is your employee-commitment profile?

It's all there in black and white.

A GOOD READ

When an employee reaches a significant years-of-service milestone (even at retirement), give each of his friends, family members and colleagues a piece of nice, scrapbook-quality paper. Encourage them to write down a note of admiration, a favorite memory of the person — anything they feel would be meaningful to the employee on this important occasion. Then gather the papers and bind them into a memory book. Believe us, it will be the best book the employee has read all year.

NOTE: This is not a last-minute project. Start well in advance — so you can be sure it gets done right.

To what extent are you willing to go?

A WINNING STRATEGY

Firms claiming to align rewards with a business strategy "to a great extent" appear to post stronger total shareholder returns (13.6 percent) than do companies that link the two to "a little extent" (9 percent) according to a Watson-Wyatt Reward Plan Survey.

So how do you create strategic rewards? Follow this simple formula:

1. Clearly communicate what you require them to do.

2. Link the reward to a business strategy.

3. Give them the skills to do the task more effectively.

4. Thank them for responding to your communication and training.

5. Start over again.

Strategic recognition is a never-ending job. Fortunately, the rewards are equally enduring.

Not for those with squeamish stomachs.

SCARY STUFF

Here's something that should give you the heebie-jeebies on Halloween. A poll by Wichita State University researchers revealed that just one in five workers has ever been publicly praised at work. Less than half of employees have ever received personal thank-yous from their bosses.

(It's enough to keep you awake at night, isn't it?)

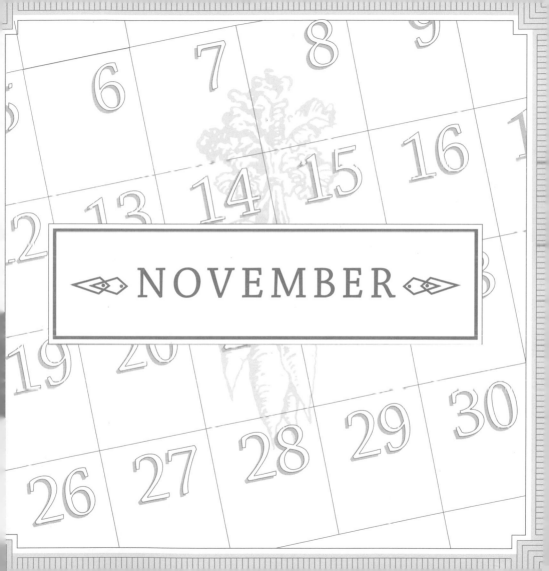

Isn't it time you got to know the relatives?

ASK ABOUT THEIR FAMILIES

Today, ask each of your employees about their children. Write down their kids' names, ages and birth dates. Then, remember those details later to become closer to your people. If some employees don't have kids, ask them about their families, parents, siblings and close friends.

You can't learn how to motivate until you learn what's important to them.

> *"The surest way to knock a chip off a shoulder*
> *is a pat on the back."*

— *Author unknown*

TURN THAT FROWN UPSIDE DOWN

We all have someone at the office who is difficult to get along with. He may become angry quickly, take offense easily or just live life with a black cloud hanging over his head (think Frank Burns). Rather than avoiding him, begin today to make a difference. It won't happen overnight, but small, consistent and sincere appreciation will eventually knock the chip right off his shoulder — allowing him to stand a little taller.

The Dirty Dozen of Why We Don't

EXCUSE NO. 11

"NO ONE HAS EVER RECOGNIZED ME!"

And two wrongs don't make a right! (Sounds eerily like your mom, we know!) If you were never recognized, that is regrettable, but it doesn't mean your people should be cheated, too. Make up for past slights and make sure your people feel good about themselves at work. Their positive feelings will spill over to their families and companions after work.

It works better than a string on your finger.

TAKE GOOD NOTES

There was something we wanted to say here. It was really important. Wait. It'll come to us. We just can't seem to remember. . . . Oh, yes. When you learn things about your people — like their birthdays or favorite restaurant or that they are vegetarians or don't drink or like dark chocolate — take notes. You think you'll remember it all, but trust us, you won't.

Some managers like to carry a small, pocket-sized notepad with them just for this purpose. Others make it a point to return to their offices and enter information into the computer. It really doesn't matter how you do it, so long as you write it down. You'll thank us later.

*"Everyone has an invisible sign hanging from their neck saying,
'Make me feel important.' "*

— *Mary Kay Ash, founder, Mary Kay Cosmetics*

READ THE SIGNS

The Cadillac of recognition has to be Mary Kay Cosmetics. (And by the way, it's a pink Caddy!) Founder Mary Kay Ash understood from the beginning that building a business means building people. She also knew that you can't give what you don't have.

That's why every lapel pin and trip and car — every single award (and there are a lot) — is designed to make employees feel important. Once they know that, they can go out and make customers feel the same way. It's a beautiful process, isn't it?

Gather the elements for recognition.

CREATE A TOOL KIT

A leading women's retailer, with about 1,000 stores around North America, was having problems with high turnover. Managers wanted to correct the problem but felt they had few tools in their arsenal to retain good employees.

A human resources associate developed a manager's recognition tool kit with a book on recognition (by a couple of guys we love), a stack of thank-you cards with envelopes, and a checkbook of fifty notes of appreciation. Managers greeted this simple tool with a standing ovation.

Today, any associate can reward a colleague by ripping off a note of appreciation from the store's checkbook. Bulletin boards are mounted in every store so employees can display the notes from peers. By the same token, managers are supplied with thank-you cards and encouraged to use them liberally.

You can check out one example of a tool kit at **www.carrotbooks.com**.

"When we feel deeply, we reason profoundly."

— *Mary Wollstonecraft, author*

PUT YOUR HEART INTO IT

You may recall the time (not so long ago) when companies commonly considered themselves family, implying that management cared about workers as people, not just producers. You may also have noticed that at some point along the way, that phrase was blacklisted by management. The unstated message was clear: we do not want to extend ourselves personally to our employees. Employees are resources. Period.

Through the years, that philosophy has trickled down to every level of business, resulting in rooms of strangers. There's just one problem with that management style: it doesn't work.

People need to know that you care. The Gallup Organization developed twelve dimensions of a highly productive work environment. Number 5 on the list of twelve is: "My supervisor, or someone at work, seems to care about me as a person."

Do the people who work for you know that you care?

When people know you care about them beyond what they produce at work, you are building emotional ties that create positive and productive workplaces.

> *"People may not remember exactly what you did*
> *or what you said, but they will always remember*
> *how you made them feel."*

— *Author unknown*

WHAT WORDS CAN'T SAY

If you sometimes worry about choosing just the right words during employee recognition moments, don't. If your mind is right and the thoughts are right, it will work out just fine. Sometimes we think we need to be great storytellers or great jokesters to make good presentations. Fortunately, we don't. The best presentations are the ones that come from the heart. Sincerity is what truly matters.

Just think of the awards you received in high school. Do you remember the exact words the presenters used? No. But right now you remember how it felt to be honored.

REMEMBER: It's how they feel, not what you say.

"To improve your self-image, do something for someone else."

— Author unknown

THE BOOMERANG EFFECT

The other day, one of us found a note slipped under the door. It was from a person we had not seen in almost a year. When I opened it, I was surprised to find a thank-you note . . . for things I had done long ago. So long ago, in fact, that I had all but forgotten them.

The timing was perfect. It had been a rough day — actually, a rough week. Reading those kinds words made me realize that although we may not see the results of our recognition efforts right away, nothing is done in vain.

I first built him up. Then he built me up. I call it the Boomerang Effect: the recognition you give away always returns to you.

When you take a closer look, it's amazing what you find.

ACTIVELY SEEK RECOGNITION MOMENTS

Now, here's a leader who truly understands the value of recognition. The CEO of one successful retailer watches weekend store receipts come in on Monday morning and then personally sends handwritten notes of praise to the best-performing managers and staff. And if an individual does something remarkable that helps meet corporate goals, he'll send a company-wide voice or e-mail recognizing that person.

The results of creating this kind of culture speak for themselves. The retailer's turnover rate is about one quarter of the industry average, sales have typically increased by 20 to 25 percent per year and the company was chosen by *Fortune* as the "Best Company to Work For in America," an honor rarely bestowed on a retail company.

When was the last time you did something ...

JUST FOR THE FUN OF IT!

On the surface, it may seem silly. It may appear frivolous. But having fun together actually pays big dividends in group cohesion.

We've heard of an international hotel that hosts an annual Thanksgiving event called "Bowling for Turkeys." At this popular activity, employees at one location gather to knock down wine bottles using frozen, duct-tape-wrapped turkeys. Organizers admit it's unorthodox, but it gets employees talking — and everyone enjoys it. In fact, they gobble it up! (Our editor rolled her eyes and groaned, too.)

Let's do lunch!

A PARTY OF TWO

Have a one-on-one lunch with an employee to thank him for a great job on a specific project. (Note: this works best if you have taken the time in advance to get to know the employee and have established a comfortable personal relationship.) At this point in the book, we probably don't need to mention who picks up the check, right?

Respect employee opinions.

THRIVE AND PROSPER

When people feel valued, companies prosper. Just look at the recent study by The Gallup Organization. Their multiyear research identified twelve key characteristics of successful workplaces — businesses in which employee retention, customer satisfaction, productivity and profitability are at high levels.

"At work, my opinions seem to count," came in at No. 7, establishing once again the link between employees feeling valued and company value.

REMEMBER: When people know that what they say matters and is making a difference, they are more engaged and more productive.

Get the family involved.

OPEN UP

Open your business to families at least one day a year, and make sure you are present and available all day to shake hands and thank employees and their loved ones in person. The more family members understand and relate to the workplace, the more supportive they can be.

Uncork the energy.

JUST BELIEVE

The business world is filled with executives just going through the motions of employee recognition. What we're talking about is entirely different.

We're talking about a leader who has risen beyond the monotony of running a recognition program to truly value employees and their contributions. And to believe in their unlimited potential.

Kent Murdock, O. C. Tanner CEO, discovered the power of believing during an extraordinarily successful corporate reorganization. He said, "I led in the best way of all. I uncorked the energy. I shouldn't get any credit, except for this: I believed in the people and I let them achieve."

Are you ready for employees to achieve? Then first you must believe.

Read all about it!

A NAME TO FAME

Extra! Extra! Read all about it! Put your high achiever in the news by submitting a story about her to her college alumni publication or hometown newspaper. It might not make Page 1, but it will make your employee feel great.

Add an extra day to her weekend

A TRIPLE PLAY (literally!)

Grant an outstanding employee a three-day weekend when she has accomplished something outstanding during the week. Make sure you help with her work while she's out.

Put recognition to the test.

TRY IT — YOU'LL LIKE IT

W ith recognition, the proof is in the pudding — and the numbers.
In a study of thirty-four organizations ranging from Universal Studios to the U.S. Postal Service, 72.9 percent of managers received the results they expected when they used non-monetary recognition either immediately or soon after the event that triggered the praise.

Put recognition to your own test. Recognize someone today.

*"If you always do what you always did,
you'll always get what you always got."*

— *Author unknown*

CAN YOU SPARE SOME CHANGE?

Wow. Déjà vu.

We are continually amazed at how long managers will put up with poor performance, low morale and high turnover before deciding that something has to change. In most cases, that something is your management approach.

Before you lose one more employee, before you have to face another quarter of disappointing profits, before one more employee comes in to complain — make a change for the better with recognition.

As they say, change is good. (Hint: prepare to be pleasantly surprised.)

You can't get there from here.

REACHING YOUR DESTINATION

Driving in rural Massachusetts, it's not unusual to stop for directions only to be told by a longtime resident, "You can't get there from here." And after being lost for hours on end, we've sometimes begun to fear they might be right.

By the same token, some things — including salaries and perks — just cannot bring you motivated employees, no matter how long or hard you try. Why? Dr. Frederick Herzberg's Motivation-Hygiene Theory has the answer.

His theory was that the opposite of job satisfaction is not dissatisfaction but, rather, no job satisfaction; and similarly, the opposite of job dissatisfaction is not job satisfaction, but no dissatisfaction.

Through his research, Herzberg identified several "hygiene" factors, which cause dissatisfaction when absent. The list includes salary and fringe benefits/perks. He found that when they are introduced, employees are no longer dissatisfied, but they are not motivated or satisfied by them either. (You just can't get there from here.)

On the other hand, Herzberg described "motivation" factors, which include recognition and sense of achievement. If these factors are present, employees are satisfied. When they are absent, employees are not dissatisfied but will lack motivation. In other words, satisfaction and motivational levels depend on these factors being present.

Find your voice.

LEAVE A MESSAGE AT THE TONE

It may not be as personal as we would like, but it can be done quickly and easily. Do it after hours so it is the first voice mail they pick up in the morning! Play some music, use funny voices; make it fun!

"At McDonald's, we believe carrots come in many forms.
We believe in treating employees with respect,
communicating openly, celebrating successes and ◆
saying thanks for a job well done."

— *Bill Johnson, President and CEO, McDonald's Canada*

LET THEM EAT CARROTS!

Double an award's impact by celebrating twice! First, with personal congratulations for the upcoming award and second, with the actual award presentation.

Bill Johnson learned this lesson when he was recognized in 1980 as one of McDonald's Canada's first recipients of the President's Award, given to the top 1 percent of McDonald's employees worldwide. George Cohon, then president and McDonald's Canada founder, called Bill into his office to tell him the great news.

Recalls Bill, "George's words of encouragement and his personal congratulations meant more to me than the award itself."

Refuel. Renew. Rejuvenate.

TAKE A FIELD TRIP

R eward your employee team with a creative field trip someplace interesting — to a museum, to a nearby landmark, to a concert, etc. Taking employees out of their routines lets them rejuvenate, so they're refueled and renewed when they return to the office.

"Success consists of a series of little daily efforts."

—*Mamie McCullough, motivational speaker*

WOULD YOU PLEASE REPEAT THAT?

Repetition is critical to getting any message across. Let us repeat that: repetition is critical to getting any message across.

That's why recognition is such a perfect vehicle for communicating your corporate vision. Each recognition moment is fresh and new and provides yet another opportunity to communicate your vision. Over time, and with frequent repetition, employees internalize your message and reinforce it daily through their behaviors. It's like broadcasting your vision in stereo. (And, frankly, that's something a wallet card or newsletter article could never do.)

Don't ruin the moment.

R-E-S-P-E-C-T

An ancient Asian belief teaches that failing to celebrate or acknowledge an achievement is to defile the moment. Show employees — and their achievements — the respect they deserve: celebrate!

"To say 'well done' to any bit of good work
is to take hold of the powers, which have made the effort and
strengthen them beyond our knowledge."

— *Philip Brooks, philosopher*

STRONGER. HARDER. FASTER.

When your mother told you that "thank you" was a magic phrase, she wasn't kidding. Just saying the words begins a process that amplifies employee abilities, commitment and motivation beyond belief.

Here's how it works: when employees see managers using their valuable time and effort to honor them, it touches their egos. (Let's be honest. Who doesn't like to be recognized?) This "shared moment" of mutual respect builds an emotional connection between the supervisor and employee. Because of that connection, the employee is willing to do more for his manager. That, in turn, strengthens the corporate culture and enables the managers to deliver more to the company through the efforts of their employees.

And the process is never ending. As managers' expectations of employees continue to rise, so does employee performance. And so on, and so on, and so on.

When you need a little magic, nothing — not abracadabra, open sesame! or even ala peanut butter and jelly sandwiches (for *Sesame Street* fans) — will do the job like a simple "thank you."

Start them on their journey.

A WELL-EARNED VACATION

A quick weekend getaway. A winter vacation in warmer climes. A day at the amusement park.

Travel communicates a very precise message to employees: that they can directly benefit from their successes. As they are lying on the beach or cruising the frozen North, the message comes through loud and clear: you are enjoying the fruits of your labors. Now, go out and do it again. (Not to mention, travel also makes spouses very fond of the company.)

NOTE FROM CHESTER: I wrote this entry while returning from a company-paid trip to Mexico. Ask me if I love my company! The answer is a resounding YES! (My wife says she does, too.)

NOTE FROM ADRIAN: The postcard Chester sent me was top-notch.

"Ability is what you are capable of doing.
Motivation determines what you do.
Attitude determines how well you do it."

Lou Holtz, football coach

THE BIG THREE

You can lead a horse to water, but you can't make him drink. And while you can hire a person with amazing talent and ability, you can't be sure she will use it to further your cause. Unless you recognize her regularly.

The big three: ability, motivation and attitude. An employee has to have them all to reach company goals. Don't drop the ball: recognize.

"Recognition is more powerful than any motivator.
Research shows that, more often than not,
cash bonuses get spent on bills and perks are soon forgotten,
but recognition becomes a memory
that is relived time and time again, continually
building higher performance."

— *Michael P. Connors, Chairman and CEO,*
VNU Media, Measurement & Information

RELIVE IT AGAIN

Michael should know. We're sure he still has flashbacks to the day he shaved his head in front of a crowd of hundreds — and made page 1 of the *Wall Street Journal.*

Believe it or not, the haircut was part of a recognition moment for Bill Polver, president and CEO of VNU's Internet subsidiary, Net Ratings. A little more than a year earlier, Mike had asked him to relocate his family of six to Tokyo to turn around the firm's Japan operations, which had been losing money for seven consecutive years.

Mike knew it was a lot to ask, so he raised the stakes. He said, "Bill, if you

continued ⇨

continuation

can turn Japan around in twelve months and you can show a profit, I will shave my head in front of everybody."

And what do you know? Bill made a profit.

So, during a leadership meeting in Spain, Mike went onstage with two barbers and had his head shaved — and it ended up in the *Wall Street Journal*, front page.

Says Mike, "Believe it or not, that was recognition. It had all the important elements: it recognized a job well done; the recognition happened in public in front of Bill's peers; it was personalized for Bill; we created a memory together that will last forever; and there was no cash involved.

(A helpful hint: for big recognition impact, incorporate these same elements the next time your employee goes above and beyond.)

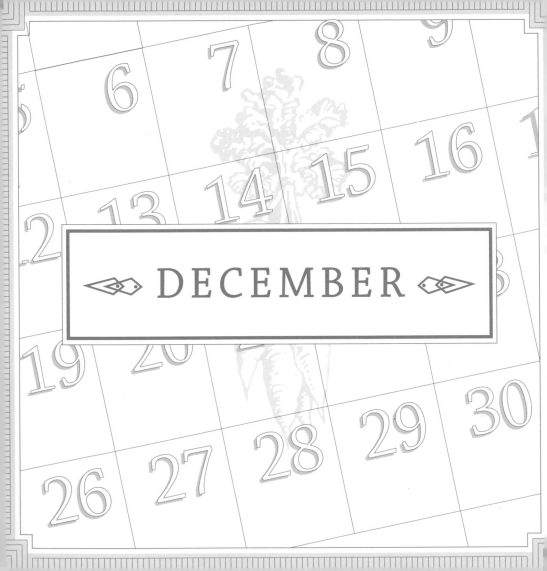

DECEMBER

Stumped?

JUST ASK

At first glance, the numbers can be a little depressing: only one third of workers believe that their employer knows what motivates them to perform well and produce high-quality work.

But then you realize that it's just the tip of the iceberg: slightly less than half of managers admit they do not know how to motivate the employees they supervise.

So what's a manager to do? Just ask them. Call in your employees one by one and ask what types of recognition they would most enjoy. It's a win-win situation. You get the answers you need; and they appreciate your attempt to better understand their needs. Not exactly rocket surgery. Or was that brain science?

December is a time of giving.

YES, YOU MUST DO SOMETHING

At this time of year, we are often asked, "Isn't the holiday party or holiday gift a bygone from the '50s?"

Well, even Scrooge danced at Fezziwigg's party, and that was certainly long before the '50s. The holiday party and gift have been around for a long time, and they'll be in place many years after we are retired to our condos in Florida.

As a manager, first, realize you must do something. Managers who try to carry on as if the holidays aren't happening can do real harm to employee loyalty. Simply put, there is no substitute for a sincere thank-you from your manager to help you feel valued and appreciated. And the holidays are the perfect time, since, frankly, employees are expecting some form of recognition.

Miss this opportunity and you give employees one more reason to look for greener pastures. The good news is, if holiday giving is done right, it can be one of the many positive memories your employees will have when the economy turns for the better and the ubiquitous headhunters start to call again.

Holiday giving should be appropriate for your work force.

FINDING THE PERFECT GIFT

One manager we talked with proudly announced she had ordered pewter bowls for her employees' holiday gifts. We asked why, given her largely male, blue-collar employee population. She sighed like we were misguided seven year olds and said, "Because everyone loves pewter bowls."

"Oh," we replied.

On our next visit, after a holiday season full of complaints from line workers, she had to admit that perhaps her assumption might have been a smidgen off base.

THE MORAL: Get to know your employees before you buy your gifts.

Be thoughtful, and consider offering a selection of items.

Make the company's gift your own.

GETTING MORE MILES FROM YOUR TURKEY

Here's a way to be generous — without spending a dime. You can get more mileage from the company's holiday gift — whether a turkey, fruit basket or cash bonus — by personally picking up those items and delivering them to your employees.

As you make the rounds with the gifts or bonuses, spend a little time with each person and express sincere gratitude for specific contributions. We guarantee the time invested will be well spent.

Avoid the pitfalls of "hamming it up."

ONE SIZE DOESN'T FIT ALL

On a radio show in New York recently, a caller told us of the well-meaning, newly hired senior leader who handed out hams to all his employees the day before Christmas — only to learn later that a good percentage of his people were Jewish.

We can all learn from his pain. When choosing holiday gifts, make sure you aren't stepping on any cultural, religious or personal taboos.

Some companies hand out "recognition questionnaires" when employees are hired — asking what occasions employees celebrate and how they like to be rewarded. Do they celebrate Christmas, Hanukkah, Kwanzaa or maybe just New Year's?

If you are asking the day before a holiday, it's too late. Plan ahead to avoid problems later.

You haven't heard the Half of it.

PULLING RANK

A ccording to research by Robert Half International, when asked which factor is most important in fostering employee satisfaction, executives from some of the country's 1,000 largest companies ranked "praise and recognition" among the top three.

Where does it rank in your priorities?

Star or middle of the road, during the holidays,
they're one and the same.

TREATING THEM EQUALLY

I f you are in charge of the official company gift, make sure gift giving is
equitable.

Holiday gifts are not to be mistaken for performance awards — where the
best employees get the best rewards. Nor should they be confused with
cash bonuses — where some people will certainly have earned more than
others. The message of a corporate holiday gift is that everyone in the organization is important to our collective success.

That doesn't mean everyone must receive the same gift, but all gifts
should be of equivalent value.

In the event that management insists on doing something special for
senior-level leaders or star performers, make sure those gifts are sent to
their homes. Otherwise, word of the inequity will spread like melted butter
on warm yams, and you'll end up looking like a turkey. Is anyone else getting hungry?

With a company gift, consistency is the name of the game.

GIFTS ARE THANKS TO THE TEAM

When people select their own awards, their satisfaction goes up. It's that simple.

This year, instead of giving the traditional turkey or other standard fare, try offering a selection of small gifts — everything from a company pen to a fruit basket and from a clock to an inexpensive yet tasteful watch.

One large pet retailer recently presented each employee with a wonderful holiday card. In the card was a message from management and a Web address and access code — allowing the recipient to go online to chose one of several useful gifts. The gifts were sent home in time for the holidays.

AN ADDED BENEFIT: The high-tech execution allowed employees' families to gather around the computer and join in on the recognition experience as well.

Avoid gift certificates like the plague.

THE FRUITCAKE OF RECOGNITION

Be sure to avoid the trap of just handing out gift certificates ("Gee, thanks. Ten bucks to spend at the Office Warehouse!). One of the biggest problems with them is that they put a dollar value on all the energy a person has expended. And you're practically guaranteed to fall short.

The response of an employee in one energy company is typical. He received his gift certificate, stuffed it into his pocket and muttered, "I worked hard for this company all year. I put in extra hours. I guess it was worth twenty-five bucks."

A thoughtful gift, on the other hand, is very hard to put a dollar figure on.

Set a time and place.

THE PARTY IS A MUST

A common mistake of managers is failing to organize a company Christmas/Holiday party. For many of your employees, the best part of the holidays is simply coming together as a group in a more relaxed setting and getting to know team members on a more personal level.

It's a manager's job to make sure the party happens. It doesn't need to be a formal affair at night. And it certainly shouldn't be the wild lamp-shade-on-the-head shindig you see in the movies. A simple lunch or potluck breakfast is all that is needed to bring people together and create some positive memories. And mistletoe is SO out.

Set spending limits for your team.

EASE THE SQUEEZE

Your employees will inevitably want to buy each other gifts at the holidays. But it's a good idea to set a limit on co\worker spending. Five to ten dollars is usually sufficient to find something appropriate — helping those with tight budgets.

Gather employees together early and ask your employees if they want to exchange serious or cheesy gifts. Letting them know you'll open the gifts at the same time will usually keep everyone on the same page.

A holiday gift provides
another opportunity to communicate.

MESSAGE IN A GIFT

Perhaps more important than your gift to employees this holiday season will be the card that accompanies it.

There is no substitute for a sincere thank-you from the company. Be sure all your communication surrounding your holiday gift is positive and thankful. The ultimate goal of the gift is to make sure employees feel valued and appreciated. After all, they are the ones keeping the doors open every day.

THE MORAL: Don't forget the card.

Remember to say thanks to your manager.

RECOGNIZING THE BOSS

We often overlook the fact that senior managers need appreciation, too. However, with that said, it's best to be frugal with holiday giving to your manager, to avoid the appearance of buying their love.

Limit your spending to a few dollars. And realize that, in most cases, your senior leader would be thrilled with a handwritten holiday card that expresses genuine thanks and lists the specific things he or she does to help you and your team succeed.

Add clients to your list.

THEY'VE BEEN GOOD ALL YEAR

A holiday gift to your client tops off the year with class. A gift basket sent to the office is usually appreciated. Unique, simple works of art are always fun. Finding your clients' favorite charities and making donations in their honor is a wonderful, personal touch. Rich Sheinaus, our book designer, gives all his clients wrapping paper he's designed.

BAD IDEAS INCLUDE: Making a donation to your favorite charity in their honor; giving expensive gifts when you are in the midst of or about to begin contract negotiations; giving very personal items like jewelry, perfume or underwear (O.K., no one would give underwear — would they?); and neglecting to do anything at all.

The Dirty Dozen of Why We Don't

EXCUSE NO. 12

"I DON'T WANT TO PLAY FAVORITES"

Oh, yes you do! The biggest reason people leave a job is lack of appreciation — and that always includes top performers. Don't lose a great employee because you are afraid of offending a mediocre member of your team. Top performers deserve all the praise and recognition you can give them. By all means, play favorites!

*"Our highest achievements come while lifting
someone else into the spotlight."*

— *Adrian Gostick and Chester Elton, authors*

POWER LIFTING

There are two ways to reach your goals: (1) pulling everyone on your team along behind, or (2) pushing them out front and letting them carry you to your ultimate destination.

Don't be afraid to build your employees or let them shine. It reflects well on your management abilities. And you'll be surprised to find that there is room enough in the spotlight for your entire team.

A reward guaranteed to make a big splash!

SEND A SEAFOOD DELICACY

Send a wonderful employee two fresh lobsters or a couple of live crabs to his home.

A picture is worth a thousand words.

SNAP AWAY!

Establish a wall of memories with photos from recognition events like picnics and softball games, service-award banquets and weddings. With digital cameras, you can take lots of photos and it costs very little. People love to see themselves in photos (despite arguments to the contrary). It's a great morale builder.

*"A mind that is stretched by a new experience
can never go back to its old dimensions."*

— *Oliver Wendell Holmes, American jurist*

EXPAND THEIR MINDS

Give people a recognition experience and the employee won't go back to old habits. And neither will you as a manager.

It's a date!

PENCIL THEM IN

Set up a calendar with all the important recognition days on it: birthdays, weddings, holidays, Administrative Professional's Day, the company picnic, service anniversaries and company anniversaries — you get the idea. It keeps important days at the forefront of your thoughts and makes it fun to plan something special.

"I spent my first few years as CEO concentrating on budgets and strategy and personnel issues, until I realized that the most important thing I and every other leader in North America must do is create the atmosphere or culture in which people work."

— *Kent Murdock, CEO, O. C. Tanner*

CREATE A CULTURAL EXPERIENCE

Disorientation. High anxiety. Feelings of alienation. Are your employees suffering from culture shock? It happens when an employee finds herself in an organization where she feels unappreciated and unchallenged.

You can change that, of course. Because you, as their leader, create the culture.

In short, if the work environment is positive, people will stay, and will stay committed. They'll drive your company forward. But if your workplace lacks employee satisfaction, you will experience turnover and a lack of productivity that will cost you money, ideas and time.

Says Jeffrey Pfeffer of Stanford University in his book *The Human Equation,* "The returns from managing people in ways that build high commitment . . . are typically on the order of 30 to 50 percent."

In your eyes, the glass should be 80 percent full.

WHEN CORRECTION IS NECESSARY

While recognition can be difficult for some leaders, correction is usually even harder.

Here's a simple formula that will make discussing performance enhancement much more positive and productive. Begin on a positive note by discussing specific areas where employee performance meets or exceeds expectations. In very precise terms, describe the one behavior that requires correction. (Resist the impulse to pile on by mentioning other failures.) Outline exactly what he is doing wrong. Then give him a detailed description of how it should be done to meet expectations. Be very explicit. End by once again expressing your appreciation for his contributions to the team.

REMEMBER: When meeting to discuss performance issues, your discussion should be 80 percent positive and only 20 percent negative.

Send them off in style.

END THE YEAR RIGHT

If employees reach milestones during the year, give them the week between Christmas and New Year's off — without having to take vacation time.

The first step is having realistic expectations.

THE MYTH OF THE WELL-ROUNDED PERSON

We'd bet you don't believe in fairies or Santa Claus (hope we didn't shatter anyone's false reality there) or the boogeyman. But there is one myth that still exists among managers: the well-rounded employee.

We sometimes want all of our people to be perfectly balanced and, frankly, it's just not realistic. It's much more productive to identify what an employee does best and turn them loose on it. Finding their niche and excelling there is good for the employee — who feels valued — as well as the company, which benefits from the employee's expertise.

Now, repeat after us: different is good.

DECEMBER
25

Recognition that really hits home.

THANKS! IT'S JUST WHAT I WANTED!

At the end of the holiday festivities, gather your children together to open one final gift: a stack of thank-you cards.

Set aside some time the following day to help them compose notes of gratitude to grandparents, friends and relatives. (If this is a new venture, you may want to give the recipients a heads up so they don't faint dead away upon receiving the cards.)

Learning the lost art of the thank-you note will serve your children their entire adult lives (particularly in management).

Recognition is no turkey.

DOUBLE, DOUBLE . . .

No more turkey. No more ham. No more divinity or fudge. The holiday season is winding up. But maybe just one more treat. . . .

Feast your eyes on these numbers: in a study of 3,000 companies, researchers at the University of Pennsylvania found that spending 10 percent of revenue on capital improvements raises productivity by 3.9 percent, but a similar investment in developing human capital (read employee recognition here) increases productivity by 8.5 percent — more than twice as much.

When it comes to boosting the bottom line, it looks like the "touchy-feely" side of business might be more like the Midas Touch.

*"Giving people a chance to be 'visible' for their work
and accomplishments is the smartest thing
a manager can do to motivate them."*

— Bits and Pieces, *publication of The Economic Press*

OUT OF THE WOODWORK

Here's something to ponder: If a tree falls in the forest and no one is there to hear, does it make a sound? And what about this one: If an employee succeeds, and no one notices, will it ever happen again?

We don't know (or care) about the tree, but the answer to the second question is clear. Employees don't do well in a vacuum. When individuals repeatedly fail to be given credit for their accomplishments, their contributions gradually fade from view.

To ensure your employees' best contributions don't disappear, give them visibility. Put them out front. Make them the heroes. Give them credit.

Do it and we guarantee you'll like what you see.

Pass the bouquet, please.

A FLOWERY APPROACH TO RECOGNITION

Looking for a great way to acknowledge a team achievement? Send a pass-along flower bouquet to your staff. Ask each employee to keep the flowers for a short time (maybe a day) and then pass them on for another staff member to enjoy.

Find out where you're at.

MEASURED SUCCESS

After you've been recognizing for a while, measure the results. Give a survey to your employees asking what they like and don't like about their work environment — and especially recognition and rewards.

Continually improve to create a place where people come and stay committed. And don't be afraid to drop us a note to let us know how you are doing.

One year down, another to go.

HOLD YOUR GROUND

Keep learning. Go online and find a recent article on employee recognition. A great place to start is **www.carrotbooks.com**.

*"There are as many ways to recognize people
as there are people to recognize.
You just have to use your brain to find them,
next time you think you've exhausted the possibilities,
THINK AGAIN . . . and again!"*

— *Eric Harvey, author*

THINK AGAIN!

This may be the end of the book, but it's just the beginning of your success through recognition. May you recognize all of your highest aspirations!